I0029428

ROBERT HARMAN

On Gestalt Therapy

A Publication of The Gestalt Journal Press

Copyright © 2006 by The Gestalt Journal Press

ISBN 13: 978-0-939266-29-6

Published by:

The Gestalt Journal Press, Inc.
290 Pond Road
Gouldsboro, ME 04607

Printed in the United States of America. All rights reserved. This book or parts thereof may not be reproduced in any form without the written permission of the publisher.

CONTENTS

Contents

Preface

This preface was written for the original, private edition of this book that was prepared as part of a celebration held when Robert Harman retired after twenty-two years as director of the Counseling Center at the University of Central Florida.

Bob Harman's first contribution to *The Gestalt Journal*, "Gestalt Marriage and Family Therapy," appeared in the second issue, published in the fall of 1978. From that point on, he was a frequent contributor and a favorite presenter at our annual conferences which began two years after the *Journal* began publication.

Bob's first contributions to professional journals that focused on Gestalt therapy were published before we began — two, "Goals of Gestalt Therapy" and "Techniques of Gestalt Therapy" were published in *Professional Psychology* in 1974. This volume includes all Bob's articles that appeared the pages of *The Gestalt Journal* over its twenty-five-year history. The final contribution, "Gestalt Therapy in the 21st Century," was his invited opening talk at a special gathering of Gestalt therapists honoring Erving Poster's and Miriam Polster's lifelong commitment to the development and growth of Gestalt therapy.

Bob was an appropriate choice to open the conference honoring the Polsters. His professional approach is similar to theirs with a focus that is always more on the clinical applications of Gestalt therapy rather than on its theoretical formulations. While not ignoring the theory, the center of Bob's attention is always on the client rather than on the canon. That focus is reflected in these articles — stories (some prefer "case studies") of clients appear in almost all.

We offer you this collection in order to make Bob's dedication to Gestalt therapy and his contributions to its clinical development a key element in this tribute to the professional facets of his life. Most of you are familiar primarily with Bob's roles within the University of Central Florida. We hope this collection will help you recognize his contributions to the professional community outside the University.

But, enough about the articles. This is not an introduction to a collection of Bob's articles, although a collection it is — one we hope he will agree to allow us to add more from other publications to in order to create a more complete collection of his writings on Gestalt therapy.

Rather, this is a tribute to a friend and colleague on the occasion of another transition in his life. Much can be said about Bob — about his dedication to things that concern him, about his sense of humor, about his laughter, about his ability to tell stories with the best, about his gentleness and, above all else, his concerns for the well-being of others.

Bob is the most unpretentious of persons. He is not one of those who goes around flashing his unpretentiousness in a manner to draw attention to themselves. He is also not one of the multitude of mental health professionals who use their skills to maintain a "one-up" position in relation to those around him. When talking with Bob about fishing, cooking, or politics, his conversation is refreshingly lacking in the "psychobabble" that has, regrettably, become a badge of our profession.

Bob Harman has mastered an art – the art of being Bob Harman. The tools he has used to create his work of art he has shared with us all – his friends, those he loves, and, most of all, his clients.

Molly Rawle
Joe Wysong
The Gestalt Journal Press

Introduction

This book was a surprise to me. It was the brainchild of Molly Rawle and Joe Wysong. In making plans for my retirement party my wife, JoAnn Alexander, asked Molly and Joe to contribute a letter or something to be presented at my retirement party. Contribute they did! The book that they put together consisted of a book containing all the articles that I had published in the *Gestalt Journal* and was presented to me when the University of Central Florida honored me upon my retirement after 22 years as their Counseling Center Director. Molly and I decided to add more articles that had been published over the years in other journals.

Molly and Joe mention, in their preface, the first two articles that I published about Gestalt therapy in 1974 in the journal *Professional Psychology.* I had submitted a manuscript too long for that journal and the editors suggested that I make it into two articles, one on theory and the other on techniques, which I agreed to do. I had originally written the manuscript because I thought that there was a paucity of articles about Gestalt therapy and I figured that I could learn as well by writing about my favorite topic. As a side note, while attending the APA convention in late summer of 1974, I met up with my friend/teacher/mentor, Jim Simkin. He mentioned having "seen" my articles. Unabashedly I asked him what he thought of them. Jim said, they are broad and not very deep and would probably appeal to graduate students. To my surprise and to Jim's, I received more than 500 requests for reprints. Requests came from every state of the union, every country in Europe, (This was before the Iron Curtain collapsed and I don't know how Bulgaria and Romania even knew of these articles.) and from Pacific Rim countries. Requesters were professors of psychology, private practitioners, counselors, social workers, etc. The enthusiastic response for these two articles started a writing career about Gestalt therapy that has spanned over 30 years.

In 1981 I was invited to submit an article about Gestalt therapy and humor to the journal, *Voices*. I accepted and was especially pleased with its publication because in the same issue of the journal was an article by Woody Allen, a decent humorist! I hope that readers got my point that I don't find humor something to be used in Gestalt therapy; rather humor flows and evolves out of the natural process of therapy. It is not something to be paraded out of a bag of tricks.

The article, "Recent Developments in Gestalt Group Therapy," published in 1984, was an attempt to inform readers about the diverse styles of Gestalt group therapy. The misunderstanding was based upon transcripts of Fritz Perls and live demonstrations by other Gestalt therapists leading workshops. Writers such as Irvin Yalom seldom looked at ongoing Gestalt groups. The misconception was that Gestalt groups were mostly individual work in the presence of others. It has been my experience that if six to ten people are put together in a group that meets weekly over time, it is impossible to stop interaction. And who would want to!

The halcyon days of Gestalt therapy in the 60s and 70s are gone forever. What is left is a dedicated group of Gestalt therapists whose debate and discussion continue to nourish and to inform those interested in our theory and methods. I hope that this book contributes to our debates and discussions.

— *Bob Harman*
Oviedo, Florida
March 2005

Volume I

Goals of Gestalt Therapy [*]

Today, many counselors are using the techniques developed by Gestalt therapists. The author explains the theory behind Gestalt therapy and discusses it in terms of its goals: awareness, maturation, integration, authenticity, behavior change, and self-regulation.

Much interest has been focused on Gestalt therapy in recent years. Training institutes are functioning in Cleveland, Atlanta, San Francisco, Los Angeles, Chicago, and Amherst, Massachusetts. Several programs about Gestalt therapy were presented at the 1972 APA Convention. Recent books by Perls (1969a) and Fagan and Shepherd (1970) have helped to make available the theory and techniques of Gestalt therapy. Gestalt therapy is a system rich in techniques. It seems that many therapists and counselors are using Gestalt techniques without much understanding of the theory, goals, or aims of Gestalt therapy. The techniques themselves may elicit intense emotional responses from clients. These responses may be potentially harmful to the client if the therapist lacks a clear understanding of the theory and goals of Gestalt therapy. The purpose of this article is twofold: first, to briefly present the theoretical founda-

[*] This article originally appeared in *Professional Psychology*, 4 (2), 1974

tions of Gestalt therapy and, second, to present and discuss the goals of Gestalt therapy.

Theory of Gestalt Therapy

Gestalt therapy is a type of psychotherapy first developed and practiced by Frederick S. Perls. Perls wrote the manuscript for his first book during the Second World War. It was published in the United States under the title *Ego, Hunger, and Aggression* in 1947. Many of Perls' basic ideas about Gestalt therapy and the nature of man can be found in this first book. However, at that time he referred to his approach as concentration therapy. The term Gestalt therapy was first used in print when Perls, Hefferline, and Goodman (1951) published a book entitled *Gestalt Therapy: Excitement and Growth in the Human Personality*. One of the reasons Perls selected the name Gestalt therapy was because of his admiration for the work of Gestalt psychologists like Kurt Goldstein, Kurt Lewin, and Max Wertheimer and their belief in the wholeness of man (Perls, 1969b).

Much of the formulation of Gestalt therapy is based in part on Goldstein's (1939) organismic theory of personality. This theory espouses the belief that normal, healthy man reacts as a whole organism, not as a disorganized, disoriented organism. This approach emphasizes the unity and integration of the "normal" personality. Any fragmentation of man is objected to. Some systems of therapy tend to deal only with the cognitive aspects of man and ignore the sensory and emotional modes of experiencing. In keeping with the organismic and existential foundation, the statement by Straus (1963) "Man thinks, not the brain" appropriately reflects the Gestalt therapy point of view.

Of special importance is the tendency of the organism to form figures and grounds. A figure is any process that emerges (becomes foreground) and stands out against a background. Put another way, figure is what the organism is paying attention to. Hall and Lindzey (1970) pointed out that, in terms of perception, figure is what occupies the center of attentive awareness. In the normal person there is a continuous flow of figures emerging from the background, fading away, or being destroyed, and something else emerging as foreground (Wallen, 1970). In other words, as new needs arise, new figures are formed. If the need is satisfied the gestalt is destroyed, permitting the formation of new gestalts.

The destruction of gestalts is one of the most important concepts in Gestalt therapy. Perls, Hefferline, and Goodman (1951) referred to this process as a kind of aggressive destructiveness and reconstructiveness. Before we can assimilate anything, some degree of destruction (destructuring) is necessary. This process should not be confused with annihilation, where the object is to wipe out something completely. Instead, in the process of gestalt destruction, the organism mounts enough aggression to close the gestalt.

This process of destroying gestalts is necessary for the healthy survival of the organism. This destruction permits the organism to absorb selectively according to its own needs. Without this process the organism is unable to pick and choose; assimilation is impossible. Interference with the formation and the destruction of gestalts may have two possible results: (a) introjection (swallowing whole) of something whether it meets the needs of the organism or not; (b) a compulsive hanging-on to the unfinished situation which results in other needs going unmet.

Aggression, when used in the content of Gestalt therapy, does not mean hostility or an unprovoked attack. Instead, aggression is viewed as a natural biological function of the organism (Perls, 1947). Perls et al. (1951) stated that aggression includes everything that an organism does to initiate contact with its environment. This kind of aggression is necessary to the health of the organism.

If a person is unable to express his aggressive impulses appropriately, that is, in making contact with the environment, it is safe to assume that they will be misused. There is no denying that aggression may be pathologically misused against objects and other persons and that it may be used against the self, as in a retroflection (Perls et al., 1951). Healthy aggression is the moving toward objects that are necessary for need satisfaction; put another way, aggression is the initiative that is needed to close gestalts or destroy figures as they form.

Without this kind of aggression the person is stuck and unable to fulfill his needs. The remainder of this article will discuss the goals of Gestalt therapy. More specifically, certain conditions are necessary for man to function as descrlbed in the first part of this article. The goals themselves are worked-for states which permit a person to function as a total organism, to form figures and grounds, to destroy gestalts, and to use his aggression appropriately.

Goals of Gestalt Therapy

The goals of Gestalt therapy can be discussed in general and in specific ways. In general terms, Simkin (J. Simkin. "An Introduction to Gestalt Therapy," unpublished manuscript, Big Sur, California,

1972.]) stated it appropriately: "My primary therapeutic task, as I see it, is to help the person I am working with accept himself." Most Gestalt therapists are in agreement with Beisser's (1970) paradoxical theory of change; that is, change occurs when one becomes what he is, not when he tries to become what he is not. So a general goal is for the client to accept himself fully as he exists right now.

Another general goal in Gestalt therapy is to help people regain or reown their potential. It is believed that many people seeking therapy have disowned or given away their own power for coping with and solving their problems. It is the goal of the Gestalt therapist to get people to do for themselves what they are capable of doing.

In specific terms, the Gestalt therapist has several goals or aims that he works toward in the therapeutic relationship. The specific goals to be discussed here are awareness, integration, maturation, responsibility, authenticity, self-regulation, and behavior change.

Awareness

Perls (1969a) believed that everything is grounded in awareness and that it is the only basis for knowledge and communication. Awareness is a state of consciousness that develops spontaneously when the organism attends to whatever becomes foreground. Awareness means being in touch with, being aware of, what one is doing, planning, and feeling. Clients are taught to be aware of how they prevent themselves from achieving certain goals they have deemed important, or of how they prevent themselves from changing behaviors they wish to change.

— ON GESTALT THERAPY —

Naranjo (1971) stated, "The immediate aim of Gestalt therapy is the restoration of awareness [p. 136]." The task of the therapist is to help the client recognize how he blocks his awareness so that he can function with all his abilities. Enright (1970) pointed out that the therapist helps the client permit his awareness to develop, thereby reestablishing the conditions under which the patient can solve his own problems. Gestalt therapists are interested in helping people become aware of "how" and "what" they are doing. When clients become aware of what they are doing in the "here and now," they are then able to make meaningful decisions and take action.

Perls (1969a) stated that awareness, by and of itself, can be curative. Sometimes it is necessary for the therapist to direct awareness by such questions as, "What's happening now?" "What are you in touch with now?" "What are you experiencing now?" These kinds of questions help to keep people in the "here and now." in order to grow, the client must be more and more aware of the self and aware of the world, instead of only in touch with fantasies, prejudices, and apprehensions. The therapist may need to direct the person's awareness to how and what he avoids in his life.

Integration

In Gestalt therapy integration has to do with the bringing together of opposites. This is helpful in that energy previously expended by two disparate parts of the person competing with each other can be brought together in a productive way. In other words, when there is competition between parts of a person, energy is drained off or neutralized. Through the integration of these parts the energy that would be lost is saved and is available for other things. Perls (1969a) felt that when opposing forces are integrated, they can join in productive combination and interplay. Also, when opposite, disparate parts are integrated, a gestalt is closed, enabling the person to move and deal with new gestalts as they are formed.

A typical example is the client who relates to the therapist that he wants to be able to express warmth and affection toward others, but a part of him prevents him from doing this. The therapist may work toward the integration of these parts by asking the client to fully identify with both parts, perhaps by developing a dialogue between the parts. Thus, the goal is integration, not the elimination of one part. Many clients are in conflict over what they "should" and "should not" do or be. This is the typical topdog/underdog dichotomy in Gestalt therapy (Perls, 1969a). The work of the therapist here is to help the client integrate his "shoulds" and "wants" so that he is able to function as a single, unified organism. It is important to remember that there is no such thing as total and permanent integration. Perls (1969a) emphasized that integration is an ongoing process.

Maturation

For the Gestalt therapist, helping people in the process of maturing is an important goal. This goal is stated very succinctly in the following quote.

> We have a very specific aim in Gestalt Therapy, and
> this is the same aim that exists at least verbally in other

forms of therapy, in other forms of discovering life.
The aim is to mature, to grow up [Perls, 1969a, p. 26].

In Gestalt therapy, maturing is the transcendence from environmental support to self-support (Perls, 1969a). The therapist will attempt to help the client learn how he prevents himself from maturing. What does he do to keep from maturing? The aim here is to get the client to furnish his own support and not depend on others to do what he is capable of doing for himself.

It is especially important for the therapist to avoid doing for the client what he is capable of doing for himself. If the therapist falls into this trap, he is helping the client to avoid standing on his own feet. Anytime the therapist does for the client what he is capable of doing for himself, he helps the client avoid maturing, avoid taking responsibility for his own life.

Perls (1970) felt a person does not mature because he does not want to take on the responsibility of the adult person. To grow up means to be alone and to be on one's own. This is a prerequisite for maturity.

Responsibility

It has been pointed out by Naranjo (1970) that responsibility is not a must but an unavoidable fact: We are the responsible doers for whatever we do. If a client wants to play the blame game and place the source of his problems on others, the goal of the therapist is to help the client become aware of and accept the responsibility for making himself feel bad by playing the blame game. The Gestalt therapist believes that when a person is aware of what and how he is doing something and accepts the responsibility for it, it is then possible for that person to decide if he wants to change his behavior. By accepting responsibility for their actions, people can become the creators of their own destinies. According to Perls et al. (1951), the aim is for the client to come to realize that he is creative in his environment and responsible for his environment — not to blame — but responsible in the sense that it is he who lets it stand or changes it. Perls (1969a, 1969b) discussed responsibility as response-ability, that is, the ability to respond. The ability to respond, to have thoughts, reactions, emotions, is taking the responsibility to he what one is. Perls went on to say that this responsibility is grounded in the word "I." Responsibility means simply the willingness to say "I am I." A favorite technique used by Gestalt therapists to encourage clients to accept responsibility for themselves is to discourage questions. Almost all questions have an implied statement or hidden agenda behind them. Very infrequently are they the uncomplicated request for information they appear to be. When a client is willing to take the risk of saying where he is and "owning" the statement behind the question, he has taken the responsibility for his actions.

Authenticity

The goal of being authentic is a strived-for state in the client; it is a must for the therapist. Being authentic means "coming on straight" and taking the risk and responsibility that goes with it. When a person is willing to state what he feels and thinks, to communicate honestly with self and others, he is being authentic.

The Gestalt therapist promotes authenticity by being the model of authenticity and direct communication. This does not mean that he impulsively or indiscriminately acts on his feelings and is completely transparent. Instead, the therapist uses selective authenticity (Cohn, 1970) and states himself in the interest of the therapeutic process. The trained therapist may decide that the revelation of certain feelings on his part could be toxic to the individual or group he is working with.

To be authentic a person must be willing to stop playing games and to stop manipulating others and the environment for the fulfillment of his wants and needs. He must be willing to ask others directly for what he wants.

Self-Regulation

Many Gestalt therapists now use the term organismic self-regulation. The belief here is that the organism is capable of selecting for itself what is nourishing; each organism has the potential for picking and choosing what is best.

According to Perls et al. (1951), if the organism is left alone, it will spontaneously regulate itself. If it has been deranged, the tendency is for the organism to right itself. The Gestalt therapist will direct the client's awareness to the total organism in the hope that the client will learn to respond to his own self-regulatory mechanisms. Simkin (1992) stated, "In the organismically balanced person, there is the capacity to experience intellectually and emotionally and sensorially." The goal of the therapist is to mobilize all three modes of experiencing so that they can be integrated as a total organism. Most patients have overstressed their "thinking about" mode of experiencing; so, much of the therapeutic work deals with the other two ways of experiencing.

Perls (1969a) described how some people ignore the preferences of the organism. He believed that the organism does not make decisions; he felt decisions to be a man-made institution. He went on to say that the organism always works on the basis of preference. The organism may designate its preference through subtle and some not so subtle ways. For example, a person may be faced with the option of doing something or not doing something; at the thought of doing this particular activity the person may develop an upset stomach, a headache, and anxiety. Because he tells himself this is something he "should" do, he makes the intellectual decision to go ahead — he ignores the organismic messages indicating the preference. Here the person is responding to a "should," which usually discounts the needs and preferences of the organism.

Behavior Change

It almost goes without saying that a goal of Gestalt therapy (or any therapy for that matter) is behavior change. Here is where the specifically stated problem of the client is dealt with. For example, a husband may say to the therapist, "I want to be able to communicate my feelings to my wife." Sometimes the successful achievement of the previously mentioned goals will result in a change of behavior; at other times it is necessary to deal directly with the behavior in question. The therapist may assist the husband by helping him become aware of how he prevents himself from the achievement of this goal; it then becomes the responsibility, of the client to decide how and what actions he is going to take.

Contrary to some forms of psychotherapy, Gestalt therapy deals with private behavior as well as public behavior. That is, the Gestalt therapist will work with people who want to change a feeling or an attitude. The achievement of this goal may or may not lead to an observable, external behavior change.

Summary

There is some overlap among the goals discussed here; work in one goal may lead to changes in other areas. For example, when the main focus of the therapeutic process has been on awareness, the client may also become more integrated and authentic. On the other hand, the client who comes to trust the self-regulatory mechanisms of the organism almost certainly becomes more aware. Also, the therapist may discover that directing awareness is a technique that helps in the achievement of one or all of the other goals. The general goals of client self-acceptance and self-support may be achieved through the attainment of one or more of the specific goals discussed here.

The theoretical beliefs in the wholeness of man, of man's tendency to form figures and ground, and the ability of man to use aggression to destroy gestalts so that new needs can be met represent the Gestalt therapy point of view of the conditions necessary for human growth. The goals described here, if achieved, will permit continued client growth.

References

Beisser, A. (1970). The paradoxical theory of change. In J. Fagan & I. Shepherd (eds.), *Gestalt therapy now: Theory, techniques, application*. Palo Alto, Calif.: Science and Behavior Books.

Cohn, R. (1970). Therapy in groups: Psychoanalytic, experiential, and gestalt. In J. Fagan & I. Shepherd (eds.), *Gestalt therapy now: Theory, techniques, application*. Palo Alto, Calif.: Science and Behavior Books.

Enright, J. (1970). An introduction to Gestalt techniques. In J. Fagan & I. Shepherd (eds.), *Gestalt therapy now: Theory, techniques, application*. Palo Alto, Calif.: Science and Behavior Books.

Fagan, J., & Shepherd, (eds.) (1970). *Gestalt therapy now: Theory, techniques, application*. Palo Alto, Calif.: Science and Behavior Books,

Goldstein, K. (1939). *The organism*. New York: American Book.

Hall, C., & Lindzey, G. (1970). *Theories of personality*. (2nd ed.) New York: Wiley.

Naranjo, C. (1970). Present-centeredness: Techniques, prescription, and ideal. In J. Fagan & I. Shepherd (eds.), *Gestalt therapy now: Theory, techniques, application*. Palo Alto, Calif.: Science and Behavior Books.

Naranjo, C. (1971). Contributions of gestalt therapy. In H. Otto & J. Man (eds.), *Ways of growth: Approaches to expanding awareness*. New York: Pocket Books.

Perls, F. (1947). *Ego, hunger, and aggression*. New York: Vintage Books.

Perls, F. (1969a). *Gestalt therapy verbatim.* Lafayette, Calif.: Real People Press.

Perls, F. (1969b). *In and out the garbage pail.* Moab, Utah: Real People Press.

Perls, F., Hefferline, R., & Goodman, P. (1951). *Gestalt therapy.* New York: Julian Press.

Perls, F. (1970). Dream seminars. In J. Fagan & I. Shepherd (eds.), *Gestalt therapy now: Theory, techniques, application.* Palo Alto, Calif.: Science and Behavior Books.

Straus, E. (1963). *The primary world of senses: A vindication of sensory experience.* Glencoe, Ill.: Free Press.

Wallen, R. (1970). Gestalt therapy and Gestalt psychology. In J. Fagan & I. Shepherd (eds.), *Gestalt therapy now: Theory, techniques, application.* Palo Alto, Calif.: Science and Behavior Books.

Techniques of Gestalt Therapy [*]

Using Gestalt techniques, the therapist can quickly reach very deep levels of emotionality. However, if he is frightened by intense emotion, these techniques should not be used.

As a psychotherapeutic system, Gestalt therapy has developed many specific techniques. The techniques permit a great deal of flexibility and are not a set of rigid guidelines that must be followed. Levitsky and Perls (1970) stressed that the techniques are definitely not intended as a set of dogmatic do's and don'ts. Some authors (Levitsky & Perls, 1970; Yontef, 1971) refer to techniques as "rules and games." The word techniques seems to be a more appropriate label because techniques imply some expertness and knowledge in the process of psychotherapy. Most of the techniques discussed here are appropriate for individual and group therapy.

Gestalt therapy techniques are not appropriate for all therapists or all patients. Fagan and Shepherd (1970) believed that therapists who have high investments in cognitive processes, who prefer

---

[*] This article originally appeared in *Professional Psychology*, (5), 1974

emotional distance, who are conservative, who prefer to reflect the patients' responses, or who lack awareness of their own experience may have difficulty with Gestalt therapy techniques. Shepherd (1970) felt Gestalt techniques should he used with caution with severely disturbed or psychotic individuals and with people who lack impulse control.

The techniques that follow are offered as possibilities for working with patients. The techniques discussed are not exhaustive; that is, the list is not complete. Techniques are limited only by the creativity of the therapist. Also, therapists will develop many different ways of using the techniques that are discussed in this article.

Exercises

Many Gestalt therapists do not make a distinction between exercises and experiments. Personally, I find it helpful as I engage in the practice of Gestalt therapy to make such a distinction. An exercise is usually an activity that is proposed to an individual or a group with some fairly specific instructions given. Frequently an exercise will have the participants withdraw into a fantasy and then share their fantasy with the rest of the group from a first-person, present-tense position as if it were happening now. Stevens (1971) introduced a rosebush identification exercise this way:

> Now I'd like you to imagine that you are a rosebush. Become a rosebush, and discover what it is like to be this rosebush. Just let your fantasy develop on its own and sec what you can discover about being a rosebush. What kind of rosebush are you? Where are you growing? What are your roots like, and what kind of ground

are you rooted in? See if you can feel your roots going into the ground. What are your stems and branches like? Discover all the details of being this rosebush. How do you feel as this rosebush? What are your surroundings like? What is your life like as this rose-bush? What do you experience, and what happens as the season changes? Continue to discover even more details about your life, and what happens to you. Let your fantasy continue for a while [p. 39].

It is up to the therapist and patient to decide what, if anything, to do with the results of the exercises. Exercises can be used to help members of newly formed groups get acquainted with each other. Usually an exercise will reveal something about the existence of the person involved. Just as in a dream, the contents of a fantasy are viewed as projections by the person. It is possible to move from an exercise to experimentation.

Experiments

More risk taking is involved in experiments because experiments usually involve going into new and unexplored territory. Experiments are proposed to an individual and seldom to the entire group, although the rest of the group may be involved in one person's experiment. Much of the activity in Gestalt therapy consists of experiments in directed awareness. (See J. Simkin, "An Introduction to Gestalt Therapy." Unpublished manuscript, Big Sur, California, 1972.) The aim is for the patient to discover how he avoids solving his own problems and how he fragments parts of himself.

Recently I was working in a group with a graduate student in education who was having real difficulty in accepting what she saw as two disparate roles for herself. One was that of a warm, caring woman; the other was that of a "hardhearted" professional. I asked her if she would be willing to experiment with this by going around to each member of the group and saying something warm, caring, and "hardhearted." As she made the rounds it became evident to her that she could integrate those two positions and did not have to be in one or the other. I recall her saying with great tenderness to one group member, "I hope you will someday claim all your masculinity." Once in a group of undergraduates a sophomore was relating how she was feeling very "small" and as if she were "sliding downhill." As she talked she described how situations and other people made her feel that way. The experiment proposed to her was that she say to each member of the group, "I am not responsible for feeling small and going downhill." As she went from person to person she became less confident in this statement; by the time she got to the last group member she was telling how she made herself feel small.

Experiments are used to confirm or disprove something doubtful, to test, to discover something unknown, and to get one in touch with his feelings (Perls, Hefferline, & Goodman, 1951). Many examples of exercises and experiments can be found in Stevens (1971) and Perls et al. (1951).

Working, Sharing, Exploring

A distinction can be made among three levels of involvement in Gestalt therapy. Working involves more risk taking than sharing or exploring. These three concepts can be used several ways. One way is to ask patients to state what they want to do; they may state, "I want to work," "I want to share," or "I want to explore." Sometimes when one is exploring or sharing he may discover something he wants to work on, or the therapist may ask him if he wants to work on something he has said. Working means that a person asks the therapist directly to work with him on a specific problem. Sharing occurs when a person shares his present awareness or an experience with the group or therapist. Exploring occurs when a person is unable or unwilling to state a specific problem, but is willing to engage in a transaction with the therapist. A patient may state, "I want to work on my inability to express love." An example of exploring might be, "I have been having this weird fantasy lately and I want to explore it." Finally, a person may share by saying, "I am experiencing a lot of warmth right now."

Staying in the "Now"

The aim of Gestalt therapy is for the patient to become aware of what he is doing at this moment. Sometimes the therapist will ask the patient to begin sentences with "Here and now I am aware of . . ." Yontef (1971) wrote that in Gestalt therapy "now" is a functional concept referring to acts done right now. When one is remembering a past experience, his "now" is remembering. Perls (1947) maintained that there is no other reality than the present. One way of getting out of the "now" is for the therapist to ask "why" questions of the patient; this is not congruent with the goals of Gestalt therapy.

Directed Awareness

Awareness means being in touch with, being aware of, what one is doing, planning, and feeling. Much of the activity of Gestalt therapy involves experiments in directed awareness. The therapist may say to a patient, "What are you aware of now?" "What is your present awareness?" "What is your now?" Or the therapist may direct the patient's awareness to some specific segment of his behavior, for example, "What is your hand doing?" "Were you aware of smiling when you told me about the rough time you had?"

Awareness is an attempt to get the patient in touch with all of himself so that he can utilize all of his potential. Through directed experiments it is possible to overcome barriers that block awareness. Perls (1969) believed that awareness by and of itself can be curative. With full awareness, a state of organismic self-regulation will develop and the person can rely on the wisdom of the organism.

Questioning

Patients are discouraged from asking questions of other patients or the therapist. Questions are rarely the simple request for information they appear to be. Usually they are disguised statements, demands for support, or attempts to manipulate others. A typical way for the therapist to handle such questions is to say to the patient, "Will you make that question into a statement beginning with the word IT." When people are willing to risk stating where they are, growth is possible. Perls (1969) wrote the following about questions:

> The way to develop your own intelligence is by changing every question into a statement. If you change your question into a statement, the background out of which the question arose opens up, and the possibilities are found by the questioner himself [p. 33].

No Gossiping

Gossiping is talking about a person in the group instead of speaking directly to him. Many Gestalt therapists will set down specific rules against this practice. In a group, the person is asked to make his statement directly to the person he is talking about. Also, when a patient talks about a person who is not present, the empty-chair technique can he used. This technique is used to promote feelings and prevent avoidance of feelings (Levitsky & Perls, 1970).

Dialogue

When a split or fragments are observed within a person, the technique of dialogue is used. The person is asked to develop a dialogue between the two parts of himself; he will actually switch back and forth from the hot seat to the empty chair as he becomes each part of the split. Frequently the split is of the top dog/underdog dichotomy (Perls, 1969). The dialogue technique can also be used to help a patient deal with a significant person who is absent (Yontef, 1971). The patient pretends the significant person is present in the empty chair and carries on a dialogue with him.

Exaggerations

In keeping with the Gestalt therapy philosophy of the wholeness of the organism, the therapist observes nonverbal as well as verbal behavior. The therapist may become aware of seemingly insignificant movements or mannerisms and ask the patient to exaggerate them. By exaggerating the movement, the inner meaning may become apparent. Recently in a group, one woman was talking (almost bragging) about how much freedom she received from her husband and children. The therapist asked her if she were aware she had made her hands into fists; she replied she was not and was asked to exaggerate this movement, Finally, as she clenched and unclenched her fists and punched at imaginary people, she shouted, "Goddamn you, pay attention to me; what do you want from me?"

The technique of exaggeration can also be used with verbal statements. A patient may have made an important statement but glossed it over, indicating he did not feel the full impact of what he said. He might be asked to repeat the statement several times, with varying degrees of intensity, until he feels the full impact of what he has said (Levitsky & Perls, 1970).

Hot Seat

The hot seat may be a real chair placed in front of the therapist; a patient indicates his desire to work by moving into it. Or, as the term is sometimes used, it indicates real work going on between the patient and therapist. This technique is effective because it promotes responsibility and commitment on the part of the patient. The patient must either move to the hot seat and say, "I want to work," or make this statement directly to the therapist from where he is seated. An empty chair is often used so that a person may fantasize significant others being there and have a dialogue with them.

Making the Rounds

When the therapist is working with a patient and notices some particular theme or topic that involves other group members, he may ask the patient to make the rounds and communicate this to each member of the group. For example, a patient was talking about his difficulty in asking directly for what he wanted from others. He was asked to say this directly to each person in the group and add any remarks he felt pertinent to his feelings about each person.

Unfinished Business

Unfinished business is the same as the incomplete gestalt. Whenever the therapist becomes aware of unfinished business or unresolved feelings on the part of the patient, the patient is asked to finish or close the situation. Resentments are the most frequently unexpressed feelings (Levitsky & Perls, 1970; Yontef, 1971). Perls (1969) maintained that the most famous of the unfinished situations is the fact that we have not forgiven and let go of our parents.

Taking Responsibility

Gestalt therapists consider all acts, thoughts, and feelings to be the responsibility of the person. Patients will often disown their own behavior. One way to handle this is to have people add, "and I take responsibility for it," at the end of each sentence, for example, "My voice is quivering and I take responsibility for it." "I am angry and I take responsibility for it." "My hands are shaking and I take responsibility for it."

Reversals

Whenever the therapist feels that a patient's overt behavior may be the reversal of some underlying feeling, the patient is asked to play the reversal. For example, the passive person is asked to play the role of a domineering person; the self-conscious person is asked to play the role of an exhibitionist; the flirtatious, seductive person might be asked to play the role of a prude, etc.

Sharing Rehearsals

Perls (1969) believed that people spend a great deal of time thinking and planning what they are going to do or say in their usual social roles. He called this rehearsing. People get stage fright and become anxious about conducting their roles correctly. Patients in therapy frequently rehearse what they want to do and say in therapy. Patients are encouraged to share their rehearsals, thereby becoming aware of how they prepare for their social roles.

"And This Is My Existence"

Frequently patients will say something very meaningful or revealing about themselves and then try to pass it off by laughing about it, denying that they said it, or claiming they were just kidding. To benefit from what they have said and to really get in touch with what they have said, the therapist might ask the person to repeat what he has said and add to the end of the sentence, "and this is my existence."

Staying with a Feeling

When reporting their awareness of unpleasant or frustrating feelings, patients show a tendency to pass over or jump from these feelings to something else, In keeping with Beisser's (1970) paradoxical theory of change, the patient is asked, "Can you stay with this feeling?" When a person gets fully into what he is, what he is feeling, then it is possible for change to take place.

Owning and Playing the Projection

Frequently when a patient talks about or to another person he is using projection. When the therapist imagines this is going on, he will ask the patient if he can own any of his statement. In the following segment taken from a group therapy session, Susan has just asked the group if they would be willing to give her some feedback about how they experience her:

> Barbara: I experience you as conceited, selfish, and as going around with your nose in the air.
> Therapist (to Barbara): How much of that can you own?
> Barbara: I don't understand.
> Therapist: If you held a mirror in front of you, how much of what you said to Susan would come back as your own?
> Barbara (very quietly): I guess I am selfish.

When a person makes a statement characterizing another person or imagines another has certain feelings, he is asked to play the other person or portray the feelings to determine if it is a projection (Yontef, 1971). The person may discover that much of what he has said about the other person is, in fact, himself. Much of what people find undesirable in others are rejected traits of their own. Levitsky and Perls (1970) reported asking the person who says to the therapist, "I can't trust you," to play the role of the untrustworthy person in order to get in touch with his own inner conflict in this area.

"May I Feed You a Sentence"

When the therapist thinks the patient has implied something or is really confused about what he is saying, he might say, "May I feed you a sentence? Try it on, see how it fits on you. Does it seem true or false?" As the patient says the sentence to the therapist or other people in a group, he is testing out his reaction to the sentence. The sentence might be rejected or it might be the key that opens a new area of awareness for the patient.

Summary

One of the strengths of Gestalt therapy is the power and number of techniques developed by its practitioners. It is possible to very quickly reach deep levels of emotionality. If the therapist is frightened by intense emotions, these techniques should not be used. Fagan (1970) cautioned against the overuse of these potent techniques and reminded therapists of other important tasks they need to be aware of. When one relies solely on techniques he becomes a technician, not a therapist.

References

Beisser, A. (1970). The paradoxical theory of change. In J. Fagan & I. Shepherd (eds.), *Gestalt therapy now: Theory, techniques, applications.* Palo Alto, Calif.: Science & Behavior Books.

Fagan, J., & Shepherd, I. (eds.) (1970). *Gestalt therapy now: Theory, techniques, application.* Palo Alto, Calif.: Science & Behavior Books.

Levitsky, A., & Perls, F. (1970). The rules and games of Gestalt therapy. In J. Fagan & I. Shepherd (eds.), *Gestalt therapy now: Theory, techniques, application.* Palo Alto, Calif.: Science & Behavior Books.

Perls, F. (1947). *Ego, hunger and aggression.* New York: Vintage Books.

Perls, F. (1969). *Gestalt therapy verbatim.* Lafayette, Calif.: Real People Press.

Perls, F., Hefferline, R., & Goodman, P. (1951). *Gestalt therapy.* New York: Julian Press.

Shepherd, I. Limitations and cautions in the Gestalt approach. (1970). In J. Fagan & I. Shepherd (eds.), *Gestalt therapy now: Theory, techniques, application.* Palo Alto, Calif.: Science & Behavior Books.

Stevens, J. (1971). *Awareness: Exploring, experimenting, experiencing.* Moab, Utah: Real People Press.

Yontef, G. (1971). *A review of the practice of Gestalt therapy.* Los Angeles, CA: California State College Press.

Gestalt Awareness Training for Graduate Students [*]

Aubrey (1973) has urged counselor educators and supervisors to present themselves as models for their students and colleagues. One way of achieving this would be to allow graduate students and colleagues to observe a counselor actually doing counseling either directly or by videotape. This idea is not particularly new, since graduate students themselves are continually asking for the opportunity to observe trained counselors at work. Graduate students are continually hearing, reading, and talking about counseling. Yet, there is little chance for them to observe a qualified counselor in action.

One way of overcoming this problem is to require counselor trainees themselves to receive counseling. This idea is usually met with opposition, since it might involve coercing or forcing people to receive counseling, and some people find it threatening to be told they have to receive counseling or psychotherapy. If the counseling is done by members of the counselor education department, the question of being open and honest with someone who is in the position of evaluating and grading becomes a valid concern.

---

[*] This article originally appeared in *Counselor Education and Supervision*, 15, (2), 1975

One viable solution to these problems is to provide Gestalt awareness training for graduate students and to have the leader be someone other than a full-time member of the department. This method will provide a role model for students and an advantage over observation in that the students themselves are involved. This type of training can be an exciting, energizing, agonizing, growing experience for the students as well as the leader. Therefore, I am proposing and will describe in this article a Gestalt awareness training program for graduate students preparing to become counselors. I will define awareness, discuss its importance, describe the way to lead an awareness group, and discuss implications of such a procedure.

Awareness

The concept of awareness is receiving increasing emphasis in several theories of counseling. Patterson (1973) mentioned awareness in his chapters on Gestalt therapy, client-centered therapy, and existential psychotherapy. An entire book has been written by Otto and Mann (1968) about approaches to expanding awareness. Historically, Gestalt therapy is the system of psychotherapy that has given the most attention to awareness. Perls, Hefferline, and Goodman (1951) have outlined eighteen experiments designed to increase awareness. Recent publications by Polster (1973) and Harman (1974) have pointed out the continued interest in awareness as a goal of counseling.

Awareness occurs when the organism spontaneously senses what arises within it. When one is aware, one is in touch with what one is doing, feeling, and wanting. When a full state of awareness develops, the organism becomes self-regulatory; one is then able to make one's own decisions and accept responsibility for them. External control, advice, and guidance become unnecessary. Thus, awareness restores the organism's ability to pick and choose what is nourishing for itself. Moreover, awareness integrates emotional and sensorial awareness, not just the intellectual awareness that so many systems of counseling and therapy pursue.

Awareness as a goal in counseling and supervision is important for several reasons. Gestalt therapists believe that wise decisions cannot be made unless they are solidly rooted in awareness. In other words, how can one make a life decision when one is aware of only a limited part of oneself. Obviously, the answer is that one cannot. When full awareness is functioning, however, one can enter into the decision-making process using one's full potential.

Awareness is the faculty that keeps one in the here-and-now, thus promoting responsibility for one's present existence. When focusing on the present, one is discouraged from making alibis, rationalizations, explanations, and justifications for one's own actions, and from blaming others. When one is remembering a childhood episode or fantasizing about getting into graduate school, remembering or planning have become that person's here-and-now. Nothing is wrong with either remembering or planning unless it prevents the person from being aware of the self and the environment. Through awareness training one learns to be in touch with three levels of awareness: awareness of self, awareness of the environment, and awareness of one's fantasies and other cognitions (Perls 1969).

Awareness training helps people become expressive rather than controlled. The Gestalt theory is that it is much more nourishing for one to express one's feelings than to attempt to control them (Greenwald 1968). The more expressive one is, the more one communicates authentically, If an individual has a strong feeling and does not express it, the feeling hangs on, interferes (sometimes blocks), and contaminates the expression of new feelings as they arise. By being aware of and by expressing what one is experiencing, it is then possible to move onto something else.

The importance of awareness applies both to counselors and clients. For example, if I am working as counselor and become aware that my attention is wandering and I am not hearing my client, I have several options. One is to try to force myself to pay attention, which usually causes a headache. A more plausible alternative is to share my awareness with the client by saying, for example, "I'm really having difficulty paying attention to you." What follows from that depends on the client. The response might be, "I was kind of bored with what I was doing," or "Are you saying I'm a boring person?" or "So what do you want me to do?" At any rate, once I have become aware of my own boredom and have shared it with the client, I find that both of our attention levels are picking up. If I am working with graduate students in counseling or leading an awareness group, several things can be observed. I have openly and honestly identified and communicated my feelings, which is something we ask the client to do. I have demonstrated that it is impossible to be interested in all clients at all times and that what I have done is one way of dealing with this problem. Furthermore, some students have told me that the sharing of self in this manner has, in their opinion, made me more human and that they find it easier to relate to me afterwards. Finally, and perhaps most important, some students reported that my sharing caused them to feel less need to be omnipotent and omniscient themselves.

It is possible to use awareness training with graduate students in several ways, and I have found students eager to participate in groups I have conducted. They seem to participate for two main reasons: to promote self-growth and to observe a Gestalt therapist "do his thing." Another way to present awareness training is to incorporate it into a seminar and give academic credit for it. Such experiential seminars give students a chance to participate in one of the most important learning experiences, that of discovering and expanding the self.

There are several positive results of awareness training. One is that the student becomes actively involved in the learning process, which is, in itself, quite energizing and exciting. Also, through expanding their awareness, they have more of their own selves available for their own lives and for their prospective clients when they start working. Awareness training is also a method by which leaders are willing to offer themselves as models for counselors, students, and colleagues.

Methods

The most frequently used method of initiating awareness training is to ask the participants to start sentences addressed to the leader with the words, "Now I am aware of . . . " Group participation is kept to a minimum at this point. In response to periods of silence the leader might say, "What are you doing now?" "What are you experiencing?" or "Are you aware of stopping?" The method may vary at this point. My preference is to ask the person to be aware of wanting to stop. I also ask the person to continue to stay with the obvious until one of us wishes to stop.

When first introduced to awareness training, people tend to do a lot of guessing and imagining. For example, one person said, "I'm aware of really concentrating on what I am doing." This is a guess about what Jim is doing, so the awareness statement becomes: "I'm aware that Jim is looking at me and I'm guessing that he is concentrating." By staying with the obvious, people learn to use and trust their senses again.

A typical first reaction among graduate students is to make this training into an assignment to be done "right" or to be done better than others do it. I point out that there is no right way to do this experiment and that it is almost impossible for the attempt to fail if one share one's awareness. Furthermore, to say "I'm aware of wanting to do this right," is the statement of a real and legitimate awareness. In later stages of awareness training statements such as this would be investigated more thoroughly and may become material to be worked on (Harman 1974).

After all group members have had the opportunity to share their awarenesses with the rest of the group (a process which might take several sessions), I introduce the different levels of awareness, pointing out awareness of one's self, one's environment, or one's fantasies (Perls 1969). Perls (1973) developed a technique he called "shuttling" to help people discover these three layers. Participants are asked to alternate starting sentences with the words "I" and "you." For example, the statement "I feel my heart pounding, you are looking at me," indicates the person is in touch with self and the environment.

The leader could ask the participants what they imagine the person looking at them is thinking. By engaging in shuttling technique, the participants become actively aware of the 'three levels of awareness.' It is not unusual at this period of training for participants to report a new awareness, that they spend most of their time in their heads fantasizing, rehearsing, thinking, planning, and so on.

As the training progresses, the leader usually becomes more active in directing awareness and in general participation. This increased activity on the part of the leader expands the awareness of the participants, and through this expansion the participants include more of their experiencing in their awareness. Another objective at this point is to help participants develop an awareness of how they block and interrupt their awareness. Frequently, the blocking is due to stories they are telling themselves. Responses such as "I will be embarrassed," "I will be scared," or "I don't think I can handle that," are commonplace. No one is forced to go beyond this point.

Those willing to go on almost always find that their catastrophic expectations are not met. That is, they find that, even if they are embarrassed or scared, they can handle it and not be overwhelmed. Many times they discover that they are not even scared or embarrassed. The point to be made here is that being scared or embarrassed are real feelings and that to avoid them prevents total growth and experiencing as a person. If counselors in training are unable to handle this type of feeling themselves they may have difficulty helping their future counselees with similar feelings.

During the latter phase the leader pays close attention to verbal and nonverbal behaviors that apparently are not within the person's awareness. For example, comments may be used such as, "Are you aware of smiling when telling me what a tough time you had?" "What are your hands doing?" "Can you hear your voice changing now?" In this way, one might be able to integrate these behaviors into one's own stream of awareness.

By broadening and expanding one's awareness, more possibilities can exist in one's professional and private life. Through awareness one can function more fully in the here-and-now; and thus have more of one's self available for helping and living.

Gestalt awareness training is one type of training model for graduate students. One of its advantages is that here students can have the opportunity to witness a fully trained professional and still be able to participate themselves. This participation is important because it not only offers some techniques and theory, but it provides a nonthreatening setting in which students can learn a great deal about themselves. This learning experience can help mobilize one's energy and excitement for living and working in the present.

References

Aubrey, R. (1973). Message to the association. *Counselor Education and Supervision, 13,* 83.

Greenwald, J. (1968). The art of emotional nourishment. Unpublished manuscript, Beverly Hills, Calif.

Harman, R. (1974). Goals of gestalt therapy. *Professional Psychology*, 5 (2) 178-185.

Otto, H., & Mann, J. (1968) . *Ways of growth: Approaches to expanding awareness.* New York: Pocket Books.

Patterson, C. (1973). *Theories of counseling and psychotherapy (2nd ed.).* New York: Harper & Row.

Perls, F. (1969). *Gestalt therapy verbatim.* Lafayette, Calif.: Real People Press. (Reprinted by The Gestalt Journal Press, Gouldsboro, ME, 1992.)

Perls, F. (1973). *The Gestalt approach/Eyewitness to therapy.* Ben Lomond, Calif.: Science and Behavior Books.

Perls, F., Hefferline, R., & Goodman, P. (1951). *Gestalt therapy: Excitement and growth in the human personality.* New York: Julian Press.

Polster, E., & Polster M. (1973). *Gestalt therapy integrated: Contours of theory and practice.* New York: Brunner/Mazel.

Gestalt Interactional Groups [*]

A frequent criticism of Gestalt groups is that they are actually individual sessions done in the presence of others. At times this is exactly the case, and our purpose here is to defend this practice as being therapeutically sound.

Since most Gestalt group leaders are interested in individuals within the group and not in the group per se, it follows that individual work is an integral part of Gestalt groups. By devoting full attention to one person, the counselor helps the client develop both a natural flow of feelings and natural ways of relating to the leader, either of which would probably be blocked or interrupted without this one-to -one involvement.

One-to-one work in a group has a number of advantages over private sessions. First, the working client is usually energized by the process of becoming the center of attention; working in front of a group can be singularly exciting. Second, the client who agrees to work in front of others is learning to take responsibility for his or her own behavior, is learning assertive behavior, and is teaming to deal with

---

[*] This article originally appeared in *Personnel and Guidance Journal*,54, (1), Sept., 1975

acceptance or rejection by others. Third, by observing group interaction, the counselor can see how an individual client interacts and can consequently direct awareness and group experience appropriately. Fourth, the non working client is given the opportunity to extract and assimilate personal meaning from the work being done. Finally, the group can be used experimentally in ways not possible in private sessions (Polster & Polster 1973). The unique experimental uses of the group is the focus of this article. Although these techniques have evolved from Gestalt therapy, we believe that counselors need not be highly trained in Gestalt therapy to integrate the techniques discussed here into their existing styles of group counseling.

We suspect that much of the criticism of Gestalt groups as one-to-one work is based on the style of Fritz Perls as reproduced in films and print. Actually, much of Perls' work as shown in his films and books is the product of workshops and does not portray ongoing counseling and therapy. Furthermore, although Perls developed much of the underlying theory of Gestalt therapy, many Gestalt therapists and counselors work quite differently in groups from the way Perls did and yet remain well within the bounds of Gestalt therapy.

Our typical way of starting a new group is to spend time during the first two sessions engaging the group in awareness exercises. After a group exercise, participants are asked to share what they experienced while they did the exercise. The unique Gestalt feature of this is that group participants are instructed to avoid labeling, giving interpretations, and making judgments. Instead, clients are asked to share as much of their awareness of themselves as they can. The dialogue reproduced below took place following an exercise in which the members of the group were asked to pair up and get to know each other without using words.

Susan: I got very excited. In fact. I still feel energy in my arms and hands.

Mary: He made me very nervous.

Counselor: Mary, could you own your nervousness and tell your partner how you experienced being nervous?

Mary: [To Bill] I got very uncomfortable when you touched my hair. I remembered Mother doing that, and 1 always got angry.

June: [To David] I enjoyed working with you; I was aware of being loose; I imagined a pleasant expression on your face.

David: I feel great! And I'm looking forward to knowing you better.

Jim: [To Susan] I felt you were being silly when you were just making sounds.

Counselor: Jim, would you be willing to own that?

Jim: Own what?

Counselor: The silly feeling.

Jim: Yeah, I felt silly, I feel silly. I want to do this right.

Exercises of this kind accomplish several things for group members: Participants' self-awareness is expanded, communication within the self (intrapersonal) is facilitated, and communication with others (interpersonal) is facilitated. When the group begins this way, several possibilities for exploration emerge. In the example above, it would be possible to work with Susan's energy, Mary's discomfort at being touched, Jim's need to be serious and do things right, and so on.

Notice that the counselors stayed out as long as they believed the participants to be authentically sharing their awareness.

One of the basic modes of Gestalt group interaction results from the Gestalt ground rule of "no gossiping" (Greenwald 1972). Group participants are asked to talk directly to other group members and not about them. This kind of encountering leads to relevant self-disclosure and more meaningful interaction. During this type of interaction we intervene only when we think coaching is necessary. It is our strong belief that interaction should be restricted when possible to authentic disclosures of feelings and thoughts. When we believe a participant begins projecting, manipulating, judging, interpreting, and so on, then we intervene.

In one group a female member said to the other participants, "Tell me what you think of me." Our previous experience indicated that this request is often a manipulation used to get others to tell the requester something nice; we intervened and asked the client to say what she really wanted from each person. She finally said, "I want you to like me." Other clients then got into an interaction with her about liking or not liking her. Through guided interaction the client was able to make meaningful contact with other group members. By establishing that contact, she worked through a personal impasse to the point where she was able to accept not being liked by everyone.

We also intervene in interactions that we feel might be harmful for one of the participants, when we believe some important aspect of behavior is going unnoticed, or when we become bored, imagine others are bored, or suspect that a natural end to the interaction has been reached. This last point is especially important from a Gestalt point of view. Our intervention is intended to assist the participants in closing and completing a gestalt. Many times group participants will stay with an interaction until it becomes stale. Instead of feeling refreshed and energized, they feel drained. So we intervene while the prospect of nourishing assimilation still exists.

Another typical mode of interaction within a Gestalt group is to use the group micro-cosmically. That is, the group can be used experimentally as a "little world" for each client. Many clients are in groups because they experience some type of interpersonal problems. For such clients the group may be used either as a laboratory in which they can achieve a deeper awareness of the mechanics of their problem or as a place where they can experiment with new ways of relating and new forms of behavior.

When a client's interaction within a group concerns an interpersonal problem, the Gestalt group leaders goal is to heighten that person's awareness of how he or she is hindering meaningful interaction. The most frequent blocks to nourishing interaction that we have encountered occur when clients believe they must be in control of themselves and others, when participants imagine that what they are really like (as revealed by true communication) would be disliked by others, and when clients tell themselves that they cannot tolerate the rejection they might experience if they were to reach out to someone else. It is our belief that people have the capacity for nourishing interaction but that by telling themselves these unfounded myths their attempts at interpersonal communication are disrupted or inhibited. In a Gestalt group we ask people first to become aware of their myths and then to test them by trying experimental behaviors within the relative safety of the counseling situation.

Another method we use, one involving the entire group, is to request each member to participate actively in something another member has started. We have found this useful when a person starts something exciting but loses the possibility of discovery by turning to depersonalizing (talking about "it"), explaining, and intellectualizing. In a recent group one member began talking about how her husband manipulated her, but she soon regressed into "talking about" manipulation. We asked her and the rest of the group if they would fantasize manipulating others and being manipulated by others and if they would share these fantasies with one another. This encounter led to an intense interaction about feelings of being manipulative in the group. It took the entire group time for that evening.

We usually announce to our groups that they may participate and interrupt at their own risk. The risk involved is that the interrupter may be perceived as abrasive and intrusive by those who are working. On the other hand, the interruption might be facilitative and valuable in assisting others through impasses and around blocks. This kind of "interrupt at your own risk" atmosphere and the ensuing feedback assists group members to become aware of the impact of their statements on others.

Group participants who are unable or unwilling to engage in this kind of group interaction rarely learn anything about themselves except when they are directly involved with the leader. They lose the possibility for discovering what it is like to have resentment or appreciation expressed directly to them. Also, group clients who impose silence on themselves are much more likely to become bored. We believe that when group members participate in the kind of group atmosphere that we are attempting to create we have achieved one of the main goals of Gestalt therapy: to teach clients to take responsibility for their own actions, feelings, and thoughts (Harman 1974).

Gestalt therapy in groups is not limited to individual work in the presence of an audience. We have described several ways in which we involve Gestalt groups interactionally. The kinds of interaction described here are well within the Gestalt framework in that they focus on learning by doing and discovering, they are non interpretive, and they respect the importance of each person's phenomenological existence. We believe that many counselors now working with groups can increase their effectiveness by incorporating the preceding techniques into their own styles.

References

Greenwald. J. 1972. The ground rules in gestalt therapy. *Journal of Contemporary Psychotherapy*, 5, 1-12.

Harman, R. 1974. Goals of gestalt therapy. *Professional Psychology*, 5, 178-184.

Polster, E., & Polster. M. 1973. *Gestalt therapy integrated: Contours of therapy and practice*. New York: Brunner/Mazel.

Recent Developments in Gestalt Group Therapy*

A gulf exists between the way Gestalt group therapy is practiced and the way it is conceptualized by some Gestalt therapists and practitioners of other theoretical persuasions. Kepner asks the question, "How has it come about that so many have mistaken the medium for the message in Gestalt therapy, and have confused the techniques and gimmicks for the essence of the method?" (1980, p. 6). This question is just as germane for group therapy as it is for individual therapy.

In spite of some excellent publications illustrating the contrary, Gestalt therapy is still conceived of by many as ". . . individual therapy in a group" (Yalom, 1975, p. 451). While the workshop method of Perls did emphasize a one-to-one (hot seat) style and discouraged group involvement in the work, what needs to be remembered is that Perls was leading workshops, not conducting ongoing therapy groups. It has been my experience, as a Gestalt therapist leading groups, that the group becomes involved. I could not stop interaction even if I wanted to.

Few Gestalt therapists insist on a "hot seat" or one-to-one approach in a group. According to Simkin: "In Gestalt therapy it is not necessary to emphasize the group dynamics, although some Gestalt

---

* This article originally appeared in *International Journal of Group Psychotherapy*, 34 (3) July 1984

therapists do. All Gestalt therapists focus at one time or another on the interactive process between the therapist and the group member in the here and now and/or the interactive process between group members as it is ongoing" (1976, p. 16). The question of group interaction is up to the therapist's individual preference and individual style. The continuum appears to consist, on the one hand, of focusing on Gestalt group process. The latter is the model espoused primarily by members of the Gestalt Institute of Cleveland (Kepner, 1980; Melnick, 1980; Zinker, 1977, 1980).

The Cleveland Model

The Cleveland model, ". . . integrates the principles and practices of Gestalt therapy and group dynamics" (Kepner, 1980, p. 5). The therapist's role is threefold: to facilitate awareness on an intrapersonal, and interpersonal, and a group level. In other words, the therapist "can function as a therapist for an individual, as a facilitator of interpersonal process, or as a consultant to the group-as-a-system" (Kepner, 1980, p. 15).

According to Kepner (1980), Gestalt groups go through three developmental stages: 1) identity and dependence, 2) influence and counter dependence, and 3) intimacy and interdependence. In the first stage, participants cope with questions about self, about others, about the leaders, and about the process. The primary task of the leader, during this stage, is to set up relationships with and among the members as quickly as possible. Skilled Gestalt group therapists will build on what is happening naturally in the group, instead of manipu-lating the process by presenting structured group exercises. At issue here is the question, "Who supplies the energy? The leader or the group members?" Structured exercises, while building confidence among the group members in the leader's ability, imply that it is appropriate for the members to "do nothing" and to wait for the leader to energize them, to liven things up. As a result, it becomes difficult for group members to move into issues that concern them since they have become dependent on the leader to supply all the fuel. My preference is to struggle along with the group's agony in not knowing what to "do" and not to provide the structured exercises that would only temporarily allay the problem. By the third or fourth session of a new group, the participants have learned that I am available, yet that I will not take responsibility for making something happen. The question to a group, "What do you want from being here?" helps solve the dependence problem. Occasionally a group member may respond, "I don't know," to which I may respond, "How is it that you don't know?" or "What's it like to not know?" Such a response sends the burden back to members to develop their awareness of what it is that they want.

The second stage in the development of a Gestalt group is called, by Kepner (1980), the influence and counterdependence stage. During this time, the group struggles with influence, authority, and control. While, in the first stage, group members try to imbue the leader with special power, now they try to take away that power. Leadership tasks during this stage include helping members become aware of the norms that are operating in the group, encouraging challenge and open expression of differences and dissatisfactions, and differentiating roles from persons. It is during this phase that group patterns and stereotyping emerge. It follows then, that the facilitation of group awareness can flourish in this second stage. In one group that I was leading, two of the members were absent; I had not been aware previously how much energy these two people were supplying until they were absent. The group that day was dull. "It appears," I commented, "that we have been depending on Ron and Bill to supply the energy for the group." We then explored how we had let this situation develop and what we wanted to do about it.

Kepner's (1980) third and final stage involves intimacy and interdependence. The newly evolved intimacy, at this stage, enables and even motivates members to deal with their differences and to struggle with their conflicts, and it is, according to Kepner, "At this stage, that members behave interdependently in the sense that they can't depend on each other for understanding, support, and challenge; also the relationships are reciprocal" (1980, p. 21). The members at this point have become comfortable with being themselves, with responding and expressing themselves as they really are. When anger emerges or when one group member "dislikes" something another member is doing, there is a sense of freedom to express the anger or the distaste. Because the group is now intimate and authentic, any expression, whether of a pleasant or unpleasant nature, is natural. It grows out of the members' integrity, not out of manipulation. The functions of the leader at this stage are to: maintain a consultative role and stay out of the way; help the group arrive at some closure; and acknowledge the unfinished business that could not be dealt with in group (Kepner, 1980).

According to Zinker (1980), Gestalt groups follow a developmental pattern much like that detailed by Yalom (1970). As Zinker and Yalom view it, the stages are: 1) superficial contact and exploration; 2) conflict and identity; 3) confluence and isolation; and 4) high cohesiveness (Zinker, 1980). Although Kepner (1980) and Zinker (1980) apply different labels to group developmental stages, the dynamics as they see them are essentially the same.

In my opinion, while they are ground breaking in their attempt to integration Gestalt therapy with group process the two articles by Kepner (1980) and Zinker (1980) are incomplete. They do not answer the question posed by Melnick: "Why move beyond the hot seat at all?" (1980, p. 89). The transcripts of groups presented by Zinker and Kepner reveal nothing unique, nothing which is not done in "traditional" Gestalt groups. Gestalt group therapists who lay no claim to integrating group process into their work could easily have facilitated the same kinds of experiences as presented in the transcripts by Zinker and Kepner. In other words, just how are "traditional" Gestalt groups different from those that marry group process with Gestalt therapy? The difference, according to Melnick (1980) and Zinker (1977), is interactional in nature. They describe "traditional" or "hot seat" kinds of groups as limiting the interaction to that between the therapist and the individual group member. When group process is integrated into the therapy, however, the interaction changes. Members interact with members. Another difference, while not dealt with explicitly by Kepner, Zinker, or Melnick, is the implied difference in therapists' beliefs about what makes behavior change possible. The Cleveland model of Gestalt group therapy advocates that the process within the group and between members are the curative factors. So in the most advanced stages of the group the leader serves as a consultant to the group, staying on the periphery out of the mainstream (Kepner, 1980). This point of view seems consistent with Yalom's position on mass group commentary: ". . . the purpose of a mass group interpretation is to remove some obstacle which has arisen to obstruct the process of the entire group" (1975, p. 174). It appears to me, and I make this interpretation cautiously, that the Cleveland model adds Gestalt therapy to group process, instead of group process to Gestalt therapy. I would prefer the latter.

Dual Focus in Gestalt Group Therapy

Gestalt group therapy has far outdistanced the "hot seat" or one-to-one style which prohibited or discouraged group participation. The articles reviewed earlier in this paper have set the tone admirably for the dynamics and growth in new directions in Gestalt therapy. In this section I will describe Gestalt therapy groups that have a dual focus. In these groups the focus is both on the individual and also on the process of the group.

There is nothing wrong with doing one-to-one work in the group. Members have things happen to them in their lives that they carry with them into group meetings and that they want to work on in group. Sometimes, the group can "help" this member work with the problem; at other times the work needs to be done, with the therapist. It is fallacy to expect, even in the advanced stages of a group's development, that it can function as its own therapist. There are times when the therapist must be more than a consultant and needs to actively work with some of the members. Gestalt therapy offers a powerful way for individuals to change their behavior and the Gestalt style of working in groups ought to be preserved along with the new emphasis on group process.

When doing one-to-one work in a group there is always the question of what the rest of the group does while one member is working. My method is to allow them to do whatever they want. For example, in the early stages of a group, members tend to sit silently while an individual works, and to give feedback once the work is finished. Frequently I hear, "I wanted to say something during the work but didn't want to interrupt." In response to this comment, I focus on helping this "non-intruder" to discover the cause of the hesitation, what beliefs, predictions, fears, and wants contributed to the reticence. Gradually the members learn that they obtain more from saying what they want to say at the pertinent time. This style helps members learn to take care of themselves at those times when they are not the center of attention and want to be involved.

At times in group, I agree to work with one person, only to find that I am busily monitoring an interaction between the original worker and other group members. Other times, I wonder aloud about what the group is doing, thinking, feeling, while the original worker and I carry on. My awareness and the group's awareness may shuttle back and forth from intrapersonal, to interpersonal, to group awareness. Group members are free to let their awareness develop in any one of these three arenas. Members learn that what they do when another works can be grist for the therapeutic mill. One group member may be "turned" off whenever the topic of parents is discussed. This realization could trigger interest in working on the "turn off." I have been in groups in which no matter what problem or situation a certain member worked on, the group consistently became bored and disinterested. Here is a perfect opportunity for such an awareness to evolve into exploration of the boredom and disinterest. What results may be a clear focus on how the entire group "agrees" to be bored and disinterested. It is always possible for one-to-one work to flow into group involvement and group interaction. Themes do develop that engulf the entire group. In one group I was leading, during a lull, I commented to a woman that she looked sad. She agreed that she did indeed feel sad and was thinking about her friend who recently died, as well as the imminent death of her grandmother. This led to an episode of intense one-to-one work revolving around loss. The rest of the group entered into the discussion. They disclosed their own feelings of losses, their feelings of the loss of group members who had dropped out, and finally the very strong feelings of loss we were all coping with about my forthcoming move to another state. This brief clinical illustration exemplifies the dual focus of one-to-one work and group dynamics. It is interesting to speculate about this particular illustration. Perhaps the one-to-one work enabled and mobilized the group to participate in the process of coping with loss and then into a more sensitive, here and now issue, the coming loss of their group leader.

At times each member of a group may be at an entirely different psychological place; at times the group may be collectively at the same place. Zinker believes that, "Each event within a Gestalt group can be characterized as a cycle" (1980, p. 56). This cycle follows a pattern of: 1) group withdrawal, rest, silence; 2) group sensation; 3) group awareness; 4) group energy; 5) group action, movement; 6) group contact; and 7) group resolution. At the point of resolution, the group then returns to the initial phase of the cycle, withdrawal. Zinker (1977) first used the cycle to describe an individual's experience, not a group's. It is descriptive of gestalt formation and destruction as first articulated by gestalt psychologists and later by Perls, Hefferline, and Goodman (1951). I have difficulty accepting parts of the cycle as Zinker (1980) describes it. Group contact and group resolution seem to me to be an individual experience within the group and not a collective one. Themes do emerge; the entire group can be energized around the same theme; yet the resolution, the destruction of that gestalt is, I believe, an individual experience.

I think that the cycle through which groups do evolve is the one described by Perls (1969) as neurotic layers: 1) cliche or phony; 2) phobic or role playing; 3) impasse; 4) implosive; and 5) explosive. When I say, "Good morning," to the janitor in my building, he responds, "Fine," before I have even said, "How are you?" We are both programmed! Newly formed groups, in this stage, stick mostly to their expected and predictable responses and are content to gather demographic data about each other. The cliche or phony layer has been described by Simkin (1976) as the "polite" or sentence layer. Group participants have a repertoire of responses that keep interaction on the surface. Behavior at this stage is robot-like and conveys little meaning.

Gestalt groups, when they move into stage two, exhibit the phobic or role-playing layer. In this stage, group members behave in their various roles; as a parent, as a bully, as a therapist, and so on. They are not really there, only the roles they present are visible (Simkin, 1976). Groups will behave as they believe they "should"; they may be supportive, quiet, antagonistic, or play whatever role they think is right.

Neither of these first two stages provides much satisfaction for the members. The leader will help the group members struggle with their frustration and lack of satisfaction. When these roles are abandoned or undermined, the group moves into stage three, the impasse. The group feels stuck, lost, empty; old habitual behaviors no longer work. Energy seems to be lacking. This is a crucial stage in the group's development. Frequently, members will drop out or at least consider doing so at this stage. While neither withdrawing nor forcing a change to happen, the leader needs to help the group cohere during the impasse. It may be helpful if the therapist verbally acknowledges to the group that this is a tough stage and that the group can move through it, not by avoiding but by focusing on being stuck. From here the group can then move into the implosive layer.

One member of my group, Fred, verbally expressed his thoughts about dropping out of group. A few others nodded in agreement but said nothing. We were in our sixth session and the group while energetic, had not experienced much depth as yet. Most of their energy had been spent in the first two stages, that is, in getting acquainted in their usual ways, playing their usual roles, and behaving as they thought Gestalt group members should. During our previous session there had been little group interest and we had stopped early. The discordant member had opened the current session by saying he wasn't getting what he wanted from the group and was thinking of dropping out. I recognized this meeting as a crucial one for this group; it was stuck at the impasse stage. My work, as I saw it, was to focus on the stuckness and how we were allowing it to happen. It was important for me not to "make" something happen. I responded directly to Fred, stating that I hadn't heard him ask for anything and that his chances of getting what he wanted out of group would increase if he could ask for what he wanted. I then directed my talking to the entire group and said I wasn't aware of many occasions where they had asked to work on anything and I would be interested in hearing how they were holding themselves back. The group became silent and fidgety. Members were looking around but not at each other. Finally, in a rush, they all began to talk, echoing familiar statements like being afraid to go first, being worried about acceptance if they disclosed their problems, and so forth. Eventually, two people asked specifically to work on their reticence, their holding back when they knew they wanted something. This illustration shows how this particular group moved through an impasse, then into the implosive and explosive level, and eventually into a theme that involved the entire group.

The implosive layer differs from the impasse in that group members experience energy, but hold it in. Clues may range from an agitated look, a fidgety movement, or a fearful expression. This stage in the group's development usually presents new territory, a chance to venture beyond the impasse. Because they are containing their energy, their excitement, the group may appear taut, on the verge of springing forth, or exploding. Perls (1969) referred to this as the dead layer, so much is being held in that the group may appear nearly catatonic. As individual members express their tensions, they will begin to explore its meaning, its direction. This often leads to group interaction and loosens everyone up.

At this point the group moves into the next stage, the explosive. Bursting into laughter, tears, anger, and so forth, the entire group is incorporated into the release. The intensity of the explosion varies, of course. At this level energy is directed outward, members feel that they have expressed something. There may be contact between some of the members, while others, not in need of contact, are privately content with the feelings of release and expression. Following this explosive stage the group will become reflective and withdrawn, as each member assimilates what has happened.

The five levels described here can be experienced in at least three ways. The group as a whole can go through this cycle, finding itself stuck on one of the levels or moving at ease past the impasse. Under the leadership of a skilled Gestalt therapist a group will usually move through these levels without feeling stymied. Advanced or more experienced groups may move right to the impasse level immediately, while beginning groups usually spend more time struggling through the cliche and role-playing layers. A veteran group member can often set the level or emotional tone from the beginning by working through individual impasses or confronting others. Another way that groups experience this cycle is to become mired. This happens when a developing theme like anger or sexuality is too threatening for the group to feel it can handle safely. Sometimes a group will become stuck in this phase because of strong feelings or fears for another member. One group member may seem much "worse off" than the rest, so the entire group defers to the person that they think "needs so much more attention than the rest." At other times one member may monopolize so much attention or be so hostile that the rest of the group inhibits itself in an attempt to stave off an attack. Once I misjudged a participant's readiness for group. In group he became disruptive, verbally attacking other members and responding belligerently to even a mild confrontation. Thus the group became stuck, nearly paralyzed, until I required the participant to switch back to individual therapy. Only then was the rest of the group able to explode into relief.

Every individual within a group does not move from level to level simultaneously. Because of the variety of individual differences and life experiences, some group members may stay stuck (for example, at the role-playing layer), while others are coping with the impasse. Therapists need to remain active so that the "stuck" member does not become the group isolate.

It is interesting to note that individual members may exist in the various individual phases while the group, on a process level, has coalesced on another stage and may move as a group through an impasse. I believe this happens as follows: the group process becomes the foreground for all of the members and offers support for the group as a whole to move. If an individual concern becomes the foreground and does not supply enough support to move, a member may remain stuck. On the other hand, sometimes one member will move through an impasse into the explosive layer and the entire group follows. In one of my groups recently, a member voiced her anger at another member. This was the first angry expression in this relatively "young" group. Individual members reported an "opening up feelings"; one even described it as feeling "like we had moved to a new level." Individuals may move with the group into confrontations or intimacy yet stay personally stuck because they believe that within the group is the only place they can experience this impasse. What stays foreground is their perceived inability to be this way in the "real world."

Conclusions

There is no doubt that Gestalt group therapy has gone beyond the "hot seat" or one-to-one style of working. Many Gestalt therapists are interested in group dynamics and the group as a whole. Both of the models presented here describe the evolution of the group. I believe that Gestalt group therapy does not have to be a choice between working with a collection of individuals or working with a group; it is, or at least it can be, both. At times the emergent gestalt is an individual, at other times it is the group.

How the therapeutic dance between the individual and the group is executed depends on the members and the style and preference of the leader. Most Gestalt therapists are lively, animated people. Some choose to direct this spirit to choreographing exercises designed to enliven and to mobilize the group, while others use their energy to help the group focus on what is happening, allowing for vibrant energy and rich themes to develop from that clear focus.

References

Kepner, E. (1980), Gestalt group process. In: *Beyond the hot seat: Gestalt approaches to group*, eds. B. Feder & R. Ronall. New York: Brunner/Mazel.

Melnick, J. (1980), Gestalt group process therapy. *The Gestalt Journal*, 3:86-96.

Perls, F. (1969), *Gestalt Therapy Verbatim*. Lafayette, CA: Real People Press.

Perls, F., Hefferline, R., & Goodman, P. (1951), *Gestalt Therapy: Excitement and Growth in the Human Personality*. New York: Julian Press.

Simkin, J. (1976), *Gestalt Therapy Mini-Lectures*. Millbrae, CA.: Celestial Arts.

Yalom, I. (1970), *The Theory and Practice of Group Psychotherapy*. New York: Basic Books.

Yalom, I. (1975), *The Theory and Practice of Group Psychotherapy.* Second Ed. New York: Basic Books.

Zinker, J. (1977), *Creative Process in Gestalt Therapy*. NY: Brunner/Mazel.

Zinker, J. (1980), The developmental process of a Gestalt therapy group. In: *Beyond the hot seal: Gestalt approaches to group*, eds. B. Feder & R. Ronall. New York: Brunner/Mazel.

Volume II

The Gestalt Journal years

Gestalt Marriage and Family Therapy [*]

In the past few years family therapy has experienced much growth, gaining acceptance by the consumer as a suitable treatment modality and by an increasing number of professionals with diverse training and background. Most graduate training programs in counseling psychology, clinical psychology, and social work now offer or require courses in marriage and family therapy. Gestalt therapy has also experienced a period of enormous growth in the past decade. There are one or more Gestalt therapy institutes in most large cities as well as in smaller ones too. Some institutes have flourishing training programs requiring a waiting period of a year before one can get in the program. While these two styles of treatment have grown, it seems to me that they have done so separately and there has not been much integration of the two. An examination of books and journals reveals a paucity of writing about the Gestalt approach to working with couples and families. The only publication I am aware of is Kempler's (1973) book, *Principles of Gestalt Family Therapy.*

---

[*] This article originally appeared in *The Gestalt Journal,* Vol. I, #2

— ON GESTALT THERAPY —

My purpose in this article is to present how I work with couples and families as a Gestalt therapist. I plan to show how I view a family from a Gestalt theoretical perspective and to explain my style of working. Time and space do not permit me to write in depth about Gestalt theory and techniques; that has been capably handled elsewhere. I will stick primarily with the techniques I use with couples and families.

Theory

In this section I will show how I adapt some basic Gestalt concepts about individual behavior and psychotherapy to the application of a family unit. The important concepts I plan to cover are homeostasis, awareness, and working in the "now." In the second part of this section I will describe the relationship of the basic Gestalt concepts to family therapy.

Basic Concepts in Gestalt Therapy

Sometimes in Gestalt therapy the process of homeostasis is referred to as organismic self-regulation. To me the terms are synonymous. This is the process whereby individuals maintain their stability and balance, their equilibrium. It is through this process that needs are met. If the homeostatic process is working when the organism is out of balance, in a state of disequilibrium, this imbalance will be experienced as a need. The need will be clear, the person does what is necessary to satisfy the need and returns to a state of balance until the next need emerges. This homeostatic process is a continuous and necessary process for all individuals. Interference with this process can result in temporary discomfort, neurosis, psychosis, even death. In other words, when this process is working the individual automatically compensates for changes in self and environment.

Awareness is another basic concept in Gestalt therapy. Awareness is an individual experience, not a family or unit happening. Individual awareness is necessary for the family to achieve the homeostasis discussed above. To be aware means to know, to be in touch with what one is feeling, planning, and thinking. In a broader sense to be aware means to know what one is doing. This includes cognizance of motives and intentions. When a person has full awareness he can be in charge of his own life, for this permits him to rely on his own organism. If he is totally aware he knows what he needs in order to satisfy himself; he does not need to rely on some external source to guide his life.

Awareness can be experienced on several levels, one being awareness of self, physically and emotionally. In this state of awareness the person is in touch with what he is experiencing. That is, the person is aware of his tension, tightness, tingling, looseness, or whatever is his physical existence.

Also, in this level of awareness, a person would be aware of his emotional state — sadness, grief, love, joy, or anger. When he experiences this level of awareness he genuinely knows "how he is."

A second level of awareness is of the world or immediate environment, accomplished by perceiving through the senses, through seeing, hearing, touching, smelling, and tasting. In this level of awareness a person discovers what is "not me." This level permits a person to discover what kind of impact he has on other people.

On a third level of awareness a person tunes into his intellect — his thinking, planning, fantasizing, explaining, and rehearsing. Fritz Perls (1969) frequently referred to this as the intermediate zone, the DMZ. Many people are operating almost exclusively in the DMZ when they come to us for therapy. Unfortunately this is the level on which much of a family's communication takes place. When people are stuck here as they frequently are, they seldom know what is going on. They are neither out in the world nor in themselves. Instead they are in their heads where events do not occur. At this level, then, people are blocking both experience and perception.

Relationship of Gestalt Concepts to Marriage and Family Therapy

Family therapists generally use the term "family homeostasis" as Jackson (1954) first introduced it: families acting in such a way as to maintain a balance in their relationships. I believe, however, families are in a state of homeostasis when needs are met, when the unit is functioning smoothly. When some need exists (either individually or collectively) this results in some imbalance in the homeostatic process. The healthy, functioning family will do what is necessary to return to a state of homeostasis, restoring balance and functioning smoothly until another need emerges. The unhealthy family experiences a disturbance in the homeostatic process in the same way a healthy one does. The difference exists in how the unhealthy family goes about restoring balance. They are unable to sense the most dominant need; they operate in a hit or miss fashion and generally remain in a state of imbalance. Many times only the needs of the dominant, assertive member of the family are met, the needs of others are suppressed.

Sometimes a family develops what I call a state of "pseudo-homeostatis." This occurs when an unhealthy family behaves as if their needs are being satisfied. On the surface they look fine. There is not much verbalized dissatisfaction. However, much is being ignored and not expressed, and usually there is a lack of sensitivity on the part of some members to others. The psuedohomeostatic family is somewhat like a closed system in that there is limited interaction with the environment. Little goes in or out and the boundaries are rigid. When families lose the ability to restore homeostasis, when unmet needs accumulate and interfere with each other, the family comes to us for therapy. I will say more about how to work with this in the next section.

A goal of the Gestalt marriage and family therapist is to develop a continuum of awareness with the couple or family, to facilitate each person's knowing when he is in contact or when he is withdrawn, when he is experiencing, and when he is in his head. Equally as important as the development of the awareness continuum is the ability to communicate this awareness to other people, a matter which I will take up later.

The awareness continuum is the foundation for much of what we do in Gestalt therapy. Remember that Perls (1969) believed that awareness per se could be curative. Once we have facilitated the awareness continuum then our patients are communicating with each other authentically. No longer are they questioning, explaining, accusing, or putting up barriers. When people are aware they are able to effectively communicate interpersonally; they develop and communicate a sense of "this is me" or "this is not me."

A well known Gestalt concept is working in the "here and now." When one is aware he is more present-centered and is not stuck in the past or future. This style of working in the "now" focuses awareness on the family as it exists right now and deters the endless, toxic pattern of blaming and fault finding.

What I have attempted to describe in this section is my view of family homeostasis and of the various levels of awareness. Homeostasis, as I see it, is a state of equilibrium and balance that exists in a family when needs are met and the family functions smoothly. When some need emerges the homeostatic process is disturbed and the family becomes dysfunctional. The awareness continuum, which assists a person in recognizing his needs, is the chief method for restoring homeostasis. If a person has full awareness he is able to distinguish and deal with each need as it emerges, while in the family situation what happens is that every member has individual needs which may be at odds with the others.' If the needs are not met and imbalance results, homeostasis can only be restored with involved in restoring awareness so that families and couples can arrive at this stage.

Style, Technique, and Application

How I use techniques depends on my "style" as a therapist; what Gestalt therapy techniques I choose to apply to family therapy depends similarly on my "style." I am somewhat bothered when people learn technique and nothing else, never drawing from the source of knowledge, the theory from which the techniques have emerged. Style, it seems, goes far beyond technique. Therapists who learn only the techniques of Gestalt therapy may give the appearance of being Gestalt therapists, but their work is superficial. In short, they have no style and when techniques fail they are lost.

Restoring Awareness

Since awareness is the foundation of Gestalt therapy it follows that I spend time working with it throughout the course of therapy and especially during the beginning phase. I am interested in how family members talk to each other. Do they look at each other? Are they talking to each other, or are they making announcements, broadcasting? Do they speak for themselves or for the group? Do they listen to each other? All of this is data to help me decide the best way to lubricate the awareness continuum. I might, as I indicated in my discussion of levels of awareness, invite them to participate in an exercise in which they share with each other the extent of their immediate awareness. At this point they would be sharing with each other what they experience physically and emotionally, what they perceive outside of themselves, and what they are doing "in their heads." During this phase I may have to direct or intervene.

Wife: (Speaking to husband) I feel you don't approve of me.
Therapist: That's not a feeling.
Wife: Well that's what I believe.
Therapist: Try saying it that way.
Wife: (Speaking to husband) I believe you don't approve of me. Yeah, that's what I mean.

Therapist: Now is there a feeling associated with that belief?
Wife: Yes, I'm tense all over.

When people learn to shuttle back and forth in their levels of awareness they have all of themselves present for communicating with each other. This opens the possibility for real person-to-person communication and not just one person's fantasies encountering another person's fantasies. So, working with the awareness continuum, I have people talk aloud to each other about how they are experiencing themselves, then switch to what they are aware of outside of themselves, then go into their heads. Interventions on my part vary. "Are you aware that you do not look at people when you talk to them?" "Did you notice that when you said you were happy you had a frown on your face?" "Tell father what you feel when you see and hear him crying right now." What I usually comment on are obvious inconsistencies, nonverbal behaviors which escape awareness, and the styles of communication employed by the family. The use of awareness will play a part in the other techniques I describe here. Without awareness not much change takes place, or the changes that take place are not particularly helpful since they do not emerge from within the person or family. Changes that occur without awareness usually include a "should" component. That is, people are responding to how they believe they should be in order to please other family members, the therapist, or some myth about what they should be like.

When family members are aware and willing to communicate their awareness to each other then they most likely will engage in a legitimate struggle. Without struggle there can be little change. Struggle need not be debilitating, something to be avoided. It can be joyful, energizing, as well as painful. Struggle is grist for the mill of change and the key is awareness.

Individual Work in the Presence of Other Family Members

I have nothing against doing some individual work in the presence of the rest of the family. In fact, there are times when I believe this is necessary. For instance, when one member does a lot of fantasizing or projecting and is not aware of it I have found that the quickest and best way to get through that is to focus attention on only that person for a while. Sometimes this comes about naturally, the flow of the therapy, concentrating on the one person, with the others fading into the background. At other times I have to invite the others to be observers while working through whatever the problem might be. Once, while working with a couple, we kept getting to the same place over and over. I believed we were doing good work, getting to the core of their difficulty, but here the wife would start crying, claiming it was too painful to continue. The husband was usually upset, became a rescuer and felt guilty. For the life of me I was not able to get past this stuck point. Finally I asked them to come together for their appointment, but I would spend half the time with her, half with him. I solicited their pledge not to interrupt. In a short time we were at the familiar place — her crying, saying "this is too painful, I'm going to pieces." I persevered, asking her where her pain was, to show me where she hurt. She demurred, saying she could not, she did not understand what I meant. I suggested that she might be storying to herself, scaring herself with threat. Again she played dumb, insisting she did not understand. I asked her to reverse what she was doing, to scare me instead of herself. She started hesitantly but began to gather steam. Her tears stopped, and her voice picked up volume, now nearly crackling with energy. She warned me I had better stop working so hard or I might develop ulcers, even suffer a heart attack. Since I was working at night I should get a guard dog, or better yet, I should start carrying a pistol in order not to get mugged on the way to my car.

When she finished her whole appearance had changed. Her eyes were bright, she had color in her face, and she was sitting up in her chair. I remarked that she looked "alive" to me for the first time. Her husband could contain himself no longer, he said it had been years since he had seen her so powerful. It had been difficult for him to stay out, to not rescue her from her helplessness. He went on to say that he now understood how he was manipulated by her crying. She was amazed at her power, how "in control" she felt. Now she was aware of how she had been scaring herself with her fantasy of "going to pieces."

I do not believe we could have gotten to this point without the individual work with her. Her husband kept his pledge to not interfere; this was crucial, and at the same time he learned something about how they were relating to each other.

Projections on the part of one family member prevent awareness and understanding of others in the family. The Gestalt "empty chair" technique can be employed in helping that person own his projections. When the individual work is finished we can then return to working with the family. I have worked with couples when both spouses are willing to come to the session but one is unwilling to participate. This is a legitimate time to do individual work while permitting the other spouse to observe. The one who is not working can learn vicariously. My experience has been that after a couple of sessions the reluctant spouse is eager to become a participant.

I am discussing giving up being a facilitator with families and taking a more active role. As a facilitator I am more or less a part of the background, doing what I can to keep the family communicating in a nourishing way. When I am more active I become foreground for at least one person, engaging him in whatever manner is necessary to work through his impasse before returning to being a facilitator again.

Interventions

Specific interventions and techniques I use are usually employed for the purpose of enhancing communication. To make the conversation between my patients more personal is one of my goals. I am interested in getting beyond the game-playing, phony role from which most people communicate. There are two important elements that make a conversation personal and thereby enhancing change. The people involved must be significant to each other and there must be some affect accompanying the words. I like Kempler's (1973) analogy that the words and music (the affect) must fit. He goes on to say, "Without words, there is only relief; without music there is only understanding." (Kempler, 1973, p. 73). So I pay attention to see if the words and affect fit, and if they are directed to the significant other. If not, then I usually intervene.

Some Gestalt therapists (Greenwald, 1972), and (Levitsky and Perls, 1970) set up "ground rules" for the group to follow and interrupt whenever there is an infringement. On the other hand, my preference is not to encumber the family with ground rules since they are already having enough trouble communicating. Instead, I wait until the appropriate moment to intervene. At the time I can give my rationale, if I am asked for it, or if I believe it necessary.

I will also intervene whenever my own homeostasis is disturbed. When my own awareness focuses on my disturbance then I must do something.

Therapist: I'm angry. I've asked a half dozen times to let one person talk at a time. Now here all four of you are bickering and arguing again. I suggest again that one of you talk at a time. I'll see that you all get a chance to talk.

This intervention expresses my anger, restores my homeostasis and the family becomes foreground for me again.

Commenting on the process of what is going on is an intervention that frequently clears up confusion and puts the family back on track.

Therapist: (Working with father, mother, and sixteen-year-old daughter) I've noticed that when mother and father are discussing something, seemingly getting closer, that you, Sarah, frequently make comments or interrupt in some way to draw their attention to you. Perhaps you have some interest in their not feeling close.

Process comments are interventions that focus on the "here and now" and help the family become more aware of what is happening.

– GESTALT MARRIAGE AND FAMILY THERAPY –

No Questions

Questions are seldom the innocent statements they appear to be. When they are legitimate requests for information I have no objection to them, but sometimes even the most harmless sounding question has some other purpose.

> Patient: Do you know what time it is?
> Therapist: Is there a statement behind that question?
> Patient: Yes, I want to leave now.

When family members and couples ask each other questions I have discovered that there is almost always a statement behind it. I look for the rest of the message and ask the person to make it into a statement. If questioning is permitted, it frequently leads to the "why/because game." The result is an intellectual trip where the answerer goes into his head and comes out with excuses, rationalizations, and justifications. These are certainly not the components of a personal conversation. As a result of questioning the answerer feels resentful, attacked, or "on the spot"; the questioner can plead innocence —"all I did was ask you a question." For the questioner this is a way of avoiding responsibility, of not taking risks.

There are times when questions serve a purpose. "What time do we meet next week?" "What are your fees?" "Could you repeat what you just said, I didn't hear you?" "Do you mean that you want a divorce?" Answers to these questions can provide clarity and missing information.

Use the Word "I"

Starting sentences with "I" leads to self-disclosure and heightens the expression of affect. Statements become much more personal than they are if started with the insipid and ubiquitous "it." Using "I" instead of "it" increases responsibility; the person no longer blames some outside source. Instead of saying "it hurts" or "you hurt me," the patient says "I hurt"; now he is involved with his own feelings.

When I suspect a person has something to say about himself and starts his sentences with "it, us, you, or they," I simply ask him to make the same statement starting with the word "I." This involves the patient more as a participant in his own struggle and takes away from the feeling that he is one to whom things are done.

Be Specific and Direct

In marriage and family therapy there is no substitute for specificity and directness. I encourage speaking directly to another person instead of to several at one time. When a person does not speak directly, what he has to say is watered down; it comes across as an announcement or a broadcast.

Father: (To no one in particular) I don't like what we are doing in this family.

Therapist: Be specific, tell each person here what they do that you don't like. When wants and needs are made specific they are out in the open and can be responded to in the same fashion.

Father: I just don't feel good when I get home from work.

Therapist: What don't you feel good about?

Father: Well the minute I get in the door she (referring to his wife) tells me something the kids have done and I'm expected to discipline them. I don't like that. I'd like to relax.

Therapist: (To wife) Can you respond?

Wife: I thought you wanted to handle the discipline.

Therapist: Did you ever ask him?

Wife: No.

When I focus on what is specific and direct I avoid getting trapped in vague, ambiguous statements that lead nowhere. Actually they lead somewhere; to confusion, frustration, and dissatisfaction. Focusing on what is specific and direct, even petty, is a starting point and also teaches a family how to talk to each other. Whatever is worked on and resolved can be replaced by something else, perhaps of greater importance.

History Taking and Diagnoses

I do not place much value in taking a family history. It is not that I believe the past to be unimportant; I believe that what is important from the past will emerge if given a chance. When a bit of history does emerge I am interested in discovering the impact it has on the family now. I then ask my clients to be aware of the past as it relates to the now. Are they using some past event to explain, excuse, or justify something in the present? If so, is it necessary? What does this help them avoid in the present? All of this is how I use past history for working in the present. What is foremost in my mind is that the only place I can intervene is in the "now." Therefore, I don't take a formal family history per se; but I do use the past as it relates to how the family is dysfunctional in the present.

Some history I treat as unfinished business. I once worked with a couple who had been married twelve years; what came out was that she was still angry at him "making" her write thank you notes the first day they returned from their honeymoon. This interfered with how she related to him in the present and had to be resolved. Unfinished business involves unresolved feelings. Some strong feeling is not expressed; usually the unexpressed feeling is one of resentment. If the unfinished business has to do with family members present for therapy then I attempt to help the family reach some sort of closure. Perhaps the unfinished business is not related to family members present for therapy; then we must develop some way for the client to finish in the present. As a Gestalt therapist my preference is to have the client recreate the situation, acting out all the parts until he feels finished. In this manner I avoid the sterility of simply being told about some past event.

Typical psychological and psychiatric diagnoses are usually of little help to the Gestalt family therapist. To label a person or family as "schizophrenic," "double-binding," or the "identified patient" does give therapists something to talk to each other about; and perhaps it creates a common language, although I have my doubts about that. Diagnoses are useful if they lead to some kind of intervention, an intervention that develops awareness and restores homeostasis. It follows, then, that the kind of diagnosing I do is process oriented; what is this couple doing right now to block their awareness and remain dysfunctional? I just finished a therapy session with a couple in which they always end a transaction with one accusing and the other defending; no matter what the topic or what I said to them, this was their pattern. They had not considered this behavior as habitual, as their style of communicating with each other. When I point this out to them that is my "in the now" diagnosis; what my diagnosis tells them is how they stop their communication. This led to my intervention which was to suggest to them that they talk to each other right now without asking questions, that they make simple statements about themselves to each other. They catch on and soon are talking to each other about their dissatisfaction with their sex life. When their questions and accusations were removed from their conversation they found some excitement in talking to each other — no small achievement!

Summary

I believe a family is dysfunctional whenever it is unable to do what is necessary to return to a state of homeostasis. From my point of view homeostasis is a wholesome condition that exists when family needs are being met. Too often families appear to be in homeostasis when on close inspection it is found that many needs are unmet. I call this a state of pseudohomeostasis; much is lurking beneath the surface.

As a Gestalt marriage and family therapist, I attempt, through the use of awareness and other techniques I have described here, to engage the family in a struggle to regain their homeostasis. The struggle is an important ingredient for without it the family remains stuck and there is no change. In fact, the family does not have to solve all of its problems, but to be struggling in a nourishing fashion is often an indication that my work is finished.

References

Greenwald, J.(1972). The ground rules in Gestalt therapy. *Journal of Contemporary Psychotherapy*, 5, 1-12.

Jackson, D. (1954).The question of family homeostasis. *Psychiatric Quarterly Supplement*, 31, 79-90.

Kemper, W. (1973). *Principles of Gestalt family therapy*. Albany, Calif.: Wordpress.

Levitsky, A. and Perls, F. (1970). The Rules and games of Gestalt therapy. In J. Fagan and I. Shepherd (eds.), *Gestalt therapy now: Theory, techniques, application*. Palo Alto, Calif.: Science and Behavior Books.

Perls, F. (1969). *Gestalt therapy verbatim*. Lafayette, Calif.: Real People Press.

Gestalt Therapy With Sexually Impotent Males:
A Holistic Approach *

Since Masters and Johnson (1970) brought the treatment of sexual problems out into the open there has been a plethora of books, articles, and workshops on techniques of treating various sexual difficulties. At the same time members of the public are no longer content to endure unsatisfactory sex lives, since just about every "slick" magazine and television talk show is telling them they can all enjoy sexual fulfillment. All of this means that more and more people are coming to therapists for treatment of sexual problems, and consequently, more and more therapists are providing services for these problems.

While most of the experts in sex therapy recommend it, treating the "whole" person who presents sexual problems remains a difficult task. Several reasons account for this: (a) there is a well-described technique for the treatment of almost every sexual dysfunction and it is easy to grasp the technique and forget about the rest of the person, (b) many patients are not open to psychotherapy and resist giving much information beyond that dealing with the content of their problem, and (c) many of the people doing the treating are not well trained in psychotherapy; since much of the

* This article originally appeared in *The Gestalt Journal*, Vol. II, #2

training in therapy and counseling consists of a "technique" approach, it is beyond their competence to provide anything else. It is a mistake to expect therapists to go beyond what they are trained to do and to be able to treat people in a more holistic manner.

I have written elsewhere about the dangers of a "technique" bound approach (1977). Here, I want to describe some cases from my practice in which it was necessary to treat the "whole person" in order to effectuate sexual potency. Gestalt therapists have long disavowed fragmentation as anti-therapeutic. Patients experience enough splitting without therapy reinforcing it by dealing only with a single sexual problem. To do so would be to ignore the ground out of which emerged the figure, the sexual problem. (For a full discussion of the figure/ground relationship in Gestalt therapy see Perls, et al., 1951). The Gestalt approach attends not only to the acknowledged problem, but also to the rest of the person and more specifically to the ways in which the person creates the problem.

A common affliction among men today, sexual impotence, falls into two categories. The first type, primary impotence, refers to men who have never been potent with women; the other type, secondary impotence, refers to those who have functioned well with women but are presently unable to perform intercourse due to erectile dysfunction. All of the men dealt with in this article suffered from secondary impotence.

Gestalt Therapy

Gestalt concepts germane to this article will be discussed. An essential component of the theory of Gestalt therapy is the concept of contact and withdrawal. When the contact/withdrawal cycle is functioning properly, a person is able to pay attention to (concentrate on) what is novel and assimilable in the environment; a clear figure emerges and the person does what is necessary to fulfill that need. The figure then fades into the background and the individual is in a state of withdrawal or stasis until this process starts over again. At times, Perls (1969) referred to this as the process of "destroying (destructuring) gestalts"; when this takes place the emerging gestalt becomes a need and is destroyed through assimilation or is rejected. In either case, the person returns to a state of withdrawal in the contact/withdrawal cycle.

In Gestalt therapy, the word "contact" usually refers to the acknowledgment of another person, while, at the same time, maintaining the sense of self. The implication here is that when a person is contactful there is a sense of what is "me and not me." Contact is usually made through one or a combination of the sensory/motor systems, sight, sound, touch, movement, and less frequently, taste and smell. When the contact/withdrawal cycle is not interrupted a person becomes aware of a need and fulfills it by having contact in one of the aforementioned ways.

Zinker (1977) has described what he calls the awareness-excitement-contact cycle, the components of which are withdrawal, sensation, awareness, mobilization of energy, action, contact, and the return to withdrawal. He states that, "The Gestalt therapist is particularly interested in bridging blockages of the awareness-excitement-contact cycle within the individual." What we know is that some people interrupt themselves at various places on this cycle. A person might interrupt before the "action" phase of this cycle, thereby not succeeding in getting much done. The Gestalt therapist will work with patients to rediscover this nourishing process of contact and withdrawal.

Awareness is the other essential component of Gestalt therapy necessary to understand when working with impotent males. Perls, et al. (1951) defined awareness as the "Spontaneous sensing of what arises in you of what you are doing, feeling, planning . . ." This implies much more than just being aware of how one feels physically. Some dilettante Gestalt therapists believe that to be aware, the patient need only say, "I'm moving my finger," "My foot is jumping," and so on. How spurious! Awareness is much broader than that. The truly aware person not only knows what he or she is doing, but also knows how he or she is doing it and what his or her intentions are.

Perls (1969) believed that awareness by and of itself could be curative. I have found that often full awareness as defined above is all that is needed in order for a patient to change his or her behavior. At other times, it is necessary, through in-therapy experiments to facilitate the development of support and skills for engaging in new behaviors by focused awareness experiments and exercises.

The Therapeutic Work

In my work I have utilized the prevalent treatment approach on non-demand pleasuring, as described by Kaplan (1974); as stated earlier, this alone did not bring lasting results. The men I worked with were still unable to make love successfully until I began to incorporate a more holistic approach to my work.

All the impotent men I have worked with share the common trait of blocking, interrupting, or in some way interfering with their expression of feelings and excitement. On the contact/withdrawal cycle (Zinker, 1977), they would block themselves before the action phase. More specifically, they would interrupt before they achieved penile insertion. This blocking tendency initiated a cycle effect which played havoc with their self-concepts and performance expectations. Generally speaking, any intimate relationship, in which sexual intercourse was a possibility, was tremendously threatening and evoked avoidance responses.

The men expressed vague feelings of threat, lack of self-confidence, and a desire to change. However, they lacked awareness of the process of how they would become impotent. Seldom did they report precisely when they lost their erections. We had to examine their experiences in detail to determine if they became impotent just prior to insertion, at the point of removing clothes, upon touching, or if they achieved an erection at all while in the presence of a potential sex partner. I believe this to be consistent with their general trait of non-awareness, non-expression, and non-sharing.

In my general treatment approach, I sought to facilitate the awareness of how and when (not why) the blocking of sexual energy occurred. One case offers a vivid example. A forty-year-old man and his wife came to me because the man had been impotent for three or four years. When I asked him to describe his latest episode of sexual impotency, in the first person present tense and in minute detail, we discovered that he would begin to lose his erection at the same time he would become aware of his wife's cologne. Further work along this line revealed that he had purchased the cologne for his wife and that it was the same kind used by a woman with whom he had an affair "three or four" years ago. The odor of the cologne almost always elicited the feelings of guilt associated with that affair and he promptly lost his erection. We worked through his guilt in therapy and his wife experimented with using a different brand of cologne or none at all. Before long he became sexually potent and active.

This kind of fantasized recreation of an attempt to make love bears further explanation. The therapist needs to pay close attention in order to be sure that the patient recreates the experience as totally as possible. We need to help the patient recover precisely what he thinks, does, and feels at the time of lovemaking. Had I not asked the patient what happened when he noticed his wife's cologne he would have skipped over it entirely. It was so unpleasant for him that he was only vaguely aware of it. So, in this kind of fantasy experiment, I would frequently ask. "What did you feel at that moment?" "What were you thinking about when that happened?" "Can you go back in time and remember the first time that ever happened?" And so on.

Usually I discover in this process not only at what point the patient becomes impotent, but also what he does to block or shift his energy. He may, for example, produce a feeling that is incompatible with the sex act, or, he may begin to make mental images of something that distracts him; or, he may talk to himself about past failures. The important point I want to make is that working with a fantasy in this style facilitates aliveness. This aliveness is more important than the fantasy technique per se; for it is this rediscovered energy on the part of the patient that makes for good therapy.

An accepted belief in Gestalt therapy involves focusing on what "is" instead of trying to "make" something happen. Translating this belief into working with impotent men means that we first develop a full awareness of what and how they are blocking before any attempt is made to implement change. By and large, the impotent men I have worked with are self-contained, that is containing (restraining) a lot of what they could express. Active retroflectors (see Perls, et al., 1951, for a full discussion of retroflection), they turn their expression and energy back onto themselves instead of turning it outward onto the significant others in their lives. As previously stated, once people are fully aware of what they are doing, change can occur. At other times, the patient needs to be committed to wanting to change after full awareness of "what is" has been developed. The following case stands out as a good example of this.

I had worked with David for six sessions and he reported no change in his sexual behavior. We had developed good rapport and trust and he reported "looking forward" to our sessions. As he rose to leave at the end of the seventh session, I noticed that he sucked in his stomach in much the same way one is taught to do in the military.

I asked him if he was aware of doing this, he smiled and said, "Yes, I want to look lean and hard to girls." When I said, "I thought you wanted your hardness to be someplace else," he looked stunned and confused. He asked me to explain. I elaborated that the energy he used to suck in his stomach might be doing two things: one, it might be draining off energy that could be used for penile insertion; and two, his tight, hard stomach might be functioning like an imaginary band that divided him into two parts and prevented feeling from flowing throughout his body. He said he understood, so I asked him if he was interested in experimenting with what we had just discovered.

Eagerly, he accepted. I suggested that he relax his stomach muscles and stand and walk around my office. He started somewhat tentatively; shortly he was chuckling deeply. I asked him what was happening and he said, "My balls are tickling me," and acknowledged this to be the first genital feelings he had experienced in a long time. This turned out to be the breakthrough we had been hoping for; this experience in therapy loosened him enough that he began to express himself in many ways to his partner. He subsequently married and continues to enjoy a satisfactory sex life. This case, I believe, highlights the Gestalt style of incorporating body awareness and experimentation in therapy.

Some impotent males place a premium on "controlling their emotions." To exhibit any strong expression of feeling is taboo. They impress me as a dour lot who from appearances do not have much fun. On the other hand, they often are successful professionally. One man, Harold, complained of his employees frequently being late for work and their work being unsatisfactory. Yet he was loath to discipline them or show his disapproval. He acted in much the same way with his wife, struggling to stay calm in the face of his impotency and her assertion that she planned to leave him. In short, Harold would not let anyone get a rise out of him. Nothing I did with Harold worked; he reported not even getting an erection during the non-demand pleasuring with his wife. Finally, she stated her plans to leave him the next week and refused to accompany him to our therapy session. During our session I asked him to fantasize that his wife was with us and to express how he felt about her leaving. At long last, he began to let himself be aware of the feelings welling up within him. He sobbed almost without control as he spoke of his love for his wife and his shame over his impotence. At the end of our session he was somewhat embarrassed at what he called his "outburst" (his term for the natural release after the buildup of tension), but reported feeling relieved. His wife called me the next morning to report that Harold had come home that night and made love to her twice. I believe his strong expression of feelings in our session helped to show him that it was a possible behavior for him. He had gone home and interacted with his wife in a contactful way. The contactful expression of feelings to a significant other is a surefire way of adding some excitement to one's life.

Contact is essential if a relationship is to have any life in it. In most cases, I believe, it is important to work with the impotent male and his partner together so that during therapy it is possible to teach them to express themselves to each other in a contactful way. Equally important, both must learn to withdraw so that the contact is not stale and draining, but enlivening.

In some ways the message the impotent male is sending to his partner is "I don't want to make love with you." The exploration of this as a possibility can be done in several ways. One is to request the male to repeat the sentence "I don't want to make love with you" to his partner and then fully explore his awareness to determine if this, in fact, is true for him. Of course this awareness may then open up many other avenues for therapy. Another way to experiment with the above possibility is to ask the patient to give his penis a voice and "speak as your penis to yourself or your partner." An example of a statement a penis might make to the partner is "I won't stand up for you." This well-known style of Gestalt enactment helps the patient become aware of material about himself that might otherwise go undetected. Goldberg (1976) has written about the "wisdom of the penis"; there are times when what a man wants is expressed more accurately through what his body does than what he says.

Summary

In this article, I have described how I have treated sexually impotent males in a holistic manner by using some of the well-known sexual exercises along with my usual Gestalt style. Due to space problems and the need for brevity I have described here only the essentials of the highlights of the work I have done. I should mention that all of the men were seen at least once after the session described, some returned for several more sessions. Nevertheless, my work as described here would have to be viewed as short term therapy. This should not be construed as obviating the need for long term therapy in some cases. The matters of primary importance in this paper are: the use of fantasy to develop full awareness of what one is actually doing; focusing on "what is" so that it is possible to discover how one is blocking contact; and using enactment as a way of discovering messages of which the patient is unaware.

References

Goldberg, H. (1976). *The hazards of being male: Surviving the myth of masculine privilege*. New York: Signet.

Harman, R. (1977). Beyond techniques. *Counselor Education and Supervision*, 17, 157-158.

Kaplan, H. (1974). *The new sex therapy*. New York: Brunner/Mazel.

Masters, W. & Johnson, V. (1970). *Human sexual inadequacy.* Boston: Little, Brown.

Perls, F. (1969). *Gestalt therapy verbatim.* Lafayette, California: Real People Press.

Perls, F., Hefferline, R., & Goodman, P. (1951). *Gestalt therapy: Excitement and growth in the human personality.* New York: Julian Press.

Zinker, J.(1977). *Creative process in Gestalt therapy.* NY: Brunner/Mazel.

Gestalt Therapy Theory: Working
at the Contact Boundaries *

Contact, a Gestalt therapy concept of utmost importance, will be the topic of this paper. I plan to define contact, support, contact boundaries, and boundary disturbances, and to offer some thoughts on doing Gestalt therapy with patients' boundary disturbances. I believe it is possible to be in contact with oneself as well as with the animate and inanimate objects in the environment. However, for the purposes of brevity, and to make this a paper instead of a book, I will deal primarily with contact of an interpersonal nature.

Contact

Gestalt therapists frequently speak of "contact." Perls, et al. (1951) provided a definition: ". . . the awareness of, and behavior toward, the assimilable novelty; and the rejection of the unassimilable novelty" (1951, p. 270). Seeing, hearing, touching, talking, moving, smelling, tasting, all are sensory motor components involved singularly, or in some combination, during contact. These allow us to contact the

---

* This article originally appeared in *The Gestalt Journal,* Vol. V, #1

actual without an interfering overlay of expectations, opinions, interpretations, and intellectualizations. Contact, therefore, is "ultimate reality" (Perls, et al., 1951, p. 85). Acknowledging, recognizing, and coping with the "other" in our existence constitutes contact. While contacting this "other," we have an awareness of what is "me" and what is "not me." When we are able to maintain our awareness of this boundary that differentiates "me" from "not me," excitement and growth are possible.

Contactful experiences occur at the boundary between the organism and its environment. More specifically, contact occurs at the boundaries between individuals. These boundary experiences are usually manifested through the sensory motor systems. At this boundary, experience occurs (Perls, et al., 1951). We must not think of the contact boundary as separating us, but rather as defining and limiting us, and at the same time, allowing us to be "in touch with" that which is not us. At this boundary we experience the novel.

The contact boundary should not be thought of as permanent or static. Instead, it has qualities of elasticity and permeability. These multifaceted properties at the contact boundary allow us to have "good" contact, but not without risk, risk that we will be rejected, that we will be enveloped or taken in, and thus lose our identities. Most of the subject matter of Gestalt therapy is made up of the possibilities, the realities of the contact boundary.

As therapists, our concern is how our patients contact other people, and how they avoid contact, for we believe contact to be "the lifeblood of growth, the means for changing oneself and one's experience of the world" (Polster & Polster, 1973, p. 101). We believe, as well, that it is exciting and energizing. This energy, when experienced in healthy contact, is expended through some form of aggression, which in the context of Gestalt therapy, does not mean hostility or an unprovoked attack (Harman, 1974). Instead, aggression is viewed by Gestalt therapists as a natural biological function of the organism (Perls, 1947), including everything the organism does to initiate contact with its environment (Perls, et al., 1951). Aggression is necessary in good contact, it must be initiated by some "step toward" (Perls, et al., 1951, p. 400) the desired object. Support is warranted in order to take this step.

Contact and Support

The consideration of contact and support helps us to understand our connectedness with Gestalt psychology, "if contact is the figure of healthy functioning in the field, support is the ground" (Latner, 1973, p. 56). Consider contact the figure and support the ground. At the contact boundary of a gestalt develops; it becomes figural. The ground provides the support for the necessary aggression or initiation to attend and complete the gestalt. Talking (one of the main contact functions) requires the support of breathing in order to be contactful. When words ride out in synchrony with exhalations, the possibility increases for reaching or contacting others. If, on the one hand, words are squeezed out muscularly, or, pushed out with too much volume, the contact possibilities diminish, since support (in this case breathing) is inadequate. Support of the legs and feet is needed in order to reach out to someone. For me, as a therapist, to listen to my patients, I must have the support of my hearing, unfettered by interpretation. In order to write this paper for instance, I call on the support of my intellect and memory; I call on my past successes in presenting papers. The expectation that I will succeed at my task provides very strong support since "Our present support depends on the success we have had in the past in carrying through the process of creating and destroying gestalts, for the past successes give us the confidence to let the process carry us on" (Lather, 1973, p. 57). Support, then, carries us to the contact boundary, toddling albeit sometimes shakily, to where contact is possible. For me, the state of child development, when a baby learns to walk, is the most fascinating; the toddler wobbles across the room, arms outreached, legs bending in every direction, finally reaching and embracing the delighted and encouraging parents. That is contact and support.

Boundary Disturbances

Contact interference or prevention, which occurs at the boundary, is known as boundary disturbance. Only in rare cases is there no contact: in severe psychosis, in certain drug states, or in the case of brain damage. Boundary disturbances we work with in therapy are experienced by our patients as "habitual," as a way of "being" in the world. These disturbances may occur with certain people, under certain conditions such as stress or, may be manifested in a fixed way in all of one's interactions with others. Boundary disturbances can also be considered as energy diversions which reduce the possibilities for encounters with others (Polster and Polster, 1973). Disturbances at the boundary usually take one or more forms: 1) retroflection, 2) projection, 3) introjection, 4) deflection, and 5) confluence. Doing to ourselves what we want to do to others or what we want others to do to us is what Gestalt therapists refer to as retroflection. Naturally, contact is impeded through retroflection, and results, at best, in contact with ourselves. What we miss in this sharp turning back on ourselves is the enlivening derived from encountering others. Retroflection may masquerade as contact; however, close scrutiny reveals otherwise. Appearing to be listening to me, some patients merely put themselves on "hold" until I finish, maybe considering their next statement, rehearsing, or thinking about something entirely unrelated to the topic at hand. While talking to themselves, retroflective patients are not available to the therapist, thus effectively excluding the possibility of contact.

A boundary disturbance which seems to have reached epidemic proportion is retroflective talking. Some patients intellectualize out loud, rather than make contact; they literally talk to themselves in our presence. In a Gestalt therapy session which I recently observed, the therapist proposed an experiment to the patient. When he finished speaking, she responded, "Are you from California?" While he had been proposing the experiment, she had been talking to herself about where the therapist was from. Other patients may talk to themselves out loud, in the therapist's presence, making the therapist a captive audience. Since I tend to resent this style of retroflection, I sometimes revert to looking at the client cross-eyed, making faces, or engaging in some other kind of outrageous behavior in order to effect contact. Sometimes the patients do not even notice me and go on with their merry chattering! While this confirms my suspicion concerning their style of disturbance, and since it does not always result in contact, I know I must initiate aggressively to meet them at the boundary. This talking is not the only way of retroflecting.

Emotions and feelings, instead of being vehicles for contact, are frequently retroflected. Some people believe that to express emotion is a sign of weakness, so they do everything possible to tamp expression. Turning emotions and feelings back on themselves, they may develop a "stiff upper lip" a "frozen pelvis," or any of a myriad of other chronic holding patterns, all of which become evident in their posture or musculature.

Some retroflectors hold in so much that they develop somatic complaints; they may complain of headache, stiffness, upset stomach. If therapists will just use the support of their own eyes, they will discover in the postural and facial expressions of their patients, a clear demonstration of the retroflection.

Another important key to uncovering the patients' retroflections is to focus attention on the words and phrases they employ. Two, especially, are classic: "I" and "myself." It is good to note the number of times you heard the phrases, "I said to myself." "I caught myself," "I want to do it myself," and so on. What develops is a retroflective split: "I" and "self." Patients nag themselves, push themselves, and punish themselves; so instead of a contact boundary that is flexible and dynamic, they produce a wall.

Energy is needed to support such a wall; therefore, one task in therapy is to help patients learn to direct this very useful energy outwardly, in some active and productive way. Since awareness is essential in undoing retroflections, patients need to know what is going on inside of them; they need a glimpse at themselves, turning their energy inward. It is especially helpful to them to discover to whom they would really like to say what they are incessantly saying. They need to know whom they would like to stroke, to cuddle; they need to know whom they would like to choke. In one of my groups, recently, one woman's voice sounded "strange" to me. I inquired about how she experienced her voice. Her response: "I feel like I'm choking." When I asked if there were someone she would like to choke, she answered, "my husband." Her words began to flow then, as she spoke to her husband experimentally, and she "let out" what she had been "choking" on.

In another experience, I noticed a group member with a little "sparkle" in his eyes. Despite his "sparkle" he was coming across as flat, dull, and frequently off-the-mark. I remembered reading in Polster and Polster (1973) about an experience in which a patient had been asked to use the therapist's name in every sentence and to point to the therapist when talking, thus effecting a very contactful interchange between patient and therapist. I tried this approach. Little happened, except that he straightened up in his chair. I then suggested that he touch, in order to emphasize points as he spoke. His whole demeanor changed. He became lively, even passionate as he tapped my chest to get his message across. He progressed to holding me by the shoulders, looking me square in the eye as he spoke. He held back nothing as he spoke to me, even telling me of his passion for trout fishing, then of his gratefulness for my sticking with him through the work. What he discovered was how he inhibited himself, limiting his expression by not allowing himself to move or touch.

These were, for me, rather dramatic cases of "undone" retroflection; however, Gestalt therapy is not always so intense. In the "I" and "myself" style of retroflection, alluded to earlier, I will some-times simply request of the patient, "say that to me," "say that to your wife," or "say that to each member of the group," thus helping the retroflector become aware of his or her divided self and then to redirecting his or her energy outward. This style of retroflective inhibition leads to stagnation; undoing it opens up fresh possibilities at the contact boundary.

Undoing all retroflections is not necessary. In fact, to do so could be disastrous. Healthy retroflection is needed for self-discipline and control (Latner, 1973). Some self-restraint is necessary in order to maintain a civilized society. On the other hand, chronically retroflective patients live in a "padded" world, insulated from contact by the walls they have constructed. Our job as Gestalt therapists is to take them back to the contact boundary where their energy can be mobilized into action. By working this way, therapists integrate retroflections, reunite divided energies so they can be discharged at the contact boundaries into the environment, where they belong (Perls, et al., 1951).

In projection, another class of contact boundary disturbance, patients disown their own traits and attribute them to other people. Projectors experience the trait or behavior as directed toward themselves, instead of from themselves. Projectors attempt to get rid of unwanted feelings, only it does not work; they still experience the unwanted feelings except now they believe it to be coming from outside themselves. Boundary disturbances, as experienced by projectors, occur when they confront the environment (Perls, et al., 1951); good contact fails to happen because projectors are mostly in touch with disowned aspects of themselves, without knowing it. Without contact with reality the projector does not develop a clear sense of "me" and "not me."

In another of my groups, no matter what Jim and Cathy told Colleen she "knew" they did not like her. When I asked her how she knew that, Colleen became confused, finally stating she "just knew." I suggested she "try on" the reverse, that she state to Jim and Cathy, "I don't like you." With that she perked up, and after saying it, spontaneously went into what she didn't like about Jim and Cathy. Invigorated by her contact with them, Colleen willingly role-played, saying all the things to herself that she had said to Jim and Cathy. This produced a surprised, "Yes, yes, yes! Those are all the things I can't stand in me." Re-owning what she had projected onto Jim and Cathy increased Colleen's grasp of herself and permitted her to have contact in a nourishing way.

In projection, just as in the other boundary disturbances, there is an interruption of the natural flow of energy necessary to form a gestalt. Projection occurs when excitement is cut off after awareness. Thus the woman who believes every man is making "passes" at her has an awareness of her sexuality, but she ascribes it to others. Projectors interrupt or inhibit their excitement so that the "I" is excluded from their experience. Therefore, some key words to listen for in order to spot projections are "they," "them," "he," "she," "you," words that deny ownership of feelings, traits, and other behaviors. In individual and group sessions, therapists need to know that what passes for feedback and other interpersonal interactions is sometimes projection and needs to be dealt with accordingly. Projections must be assimilated before contact can occur.

There are other kinds of projection and not all are negative or non-contactful. Artists project parts of themselves onto their canvases, composers into their music. Some degree of projecting into the future is necessary for planning. For me to finish this paper on time I need to anticipate how much time I will need to write it, and plan accordingly.

Working with projectors is founded upon aiding them in reowning their identities. Restoring to them a sense of power and energy so that they experience the "I" of their existence is essential.

Through the process of introjection, people take in beliefs, values, and feelings from others. This material is not assimilated and is not integrated into the personality. Gestalt therapists frequently find introjection to be analogous to eating. When a piece of food is swallowed without being chewed, it lies in the stomach, causes dyspepsia, and passes on through the system without giving much nourishment. Introjectors swallow things they don't like (because it is "good" for them) and then feel "poisoned." They are unable to digest what they've swallowed and may eventually even vomit it back up. There is little, if any, assimilation and the "food" is expelled, whole, without being destroyed, or even altered.

Introjectors report experiencing themselves as phony, superficial, automatic and distant from people; and it is not unusual for others to have similar impressions of them. Introjectors make poor contact as they have difficulty developing a sense of "me" and "not me." Boundary experiences can be almost nonexistent for them. They hove token in so much from others that they have little sense of self-identity.

Key personality traits of introjectors are impatience and greed. They want immediate gratification without having to "chew" through something. "Gestalt therapists" in the late 60's often introjected Fritz Perls' techniques, without properly chewing through Gestalt theory. Identity problems are rampant for introjectors since much of their behavior does not really belong to them.

The perceptive Gestalt therapist will recognize introjectors by their compliance. Introjectors experiment willingly, yet get little from it. They get what they think they should get, parroting the "good patient." Since they tend to "swallow whole," without chewing or evaluating, they seldom discover if the material suits them or not. Since introjectors are so solicitous, Gestalt therapists must be particularly careful to avoid giving advice to them.

Of primary importance when working with introjectors is establishing a firm sense of boundary, or what is "me" and "not me." Working with a group member, Mike, I began to suspect that he was taking in everything I said without discriminating, so I suggested that he stand up, sit down, stand up, sit down, and so on. This went on for several minutes, by now the rest of the group having caught on. Finally Mike said, "No, I won't do this anymore." This experience permitted Mike to make a choice and to experience a sense of self-identity. Any kind of interaction in which the introjector makes "I" statements may help undo the introjection.

Deflection was first introduced into Gestalt therapy literature as "a maneuver for turning aside from direct contact with another person" (Polster and Polster, 1973, p. 89). As a boundary disturbance, deflection is used to interfere with contact by both receivers and senders of messages. Senders put out their messages with a "scatter-gun" effect; sometimes they hit the target, if they aim in the right direction, while at other times their message may miss its target entirely. Receivers deflect contact with armored consistency so that few messages have impact on them.

In deflection the person deflects or in some way defuses possible contact. Words from others seem to have little effect; they ricochet off as if from invisible shields. Deflections serve to "water down" feelings; not only do they weaken the impact of others, but they also sap the vitality of responding. In group, deflectors' responses will often seem inappropriate or out of context; they may seem confused and "off the mark." Recently, in a group therapy session, a divorced man was disclosing the agony he experienced each time he said goodbye after visiting his children. One group member proceeded to ask him how many children he had, another how often he visited them and the therapist-in-training how old they were. These deflections helped ward off whatever feelings were being aroused in the group members, even in the therapist. The man may also have been led from experiencing and working through his feelings to a rather ineffective "talking about" level of interaction.

In the early developmental stages of a group, deflection and projection will be particularly pervasive. The group leader then needs a keen awareness during early group sessions, in order to intervene when necessary, facilitating the reowning of feelings, and establishing contact between patients. This is not to say that projection and deflection do not occur throughout all the stages of a group; they do. It is just that these ways of interfering with contact tend to surface early and must be dealt with effectively if the group is to progress.

Useful purposes may be served by deflection. At least some of the time it is considered healthy. Deflection can take the heat out of our responses, so that it is possible for us to remain in contact and not to withdraw or, in extreme cases, attack. Deflection enables us not to respond to all the stimuli that impinge upon us.

Doing therapy with deflectors requires helping patients establish contact in order to add zest and freshness to their interactions. This can be done in many ways. First of all, the Gestalt therapist must be willing to ask, tease, cajole, provoke, or demand contact from patients. In responding, the deflector begins to experience the contact boundary as an energizing, exciting place to be. Polster and Polster (1973) report asking a patient to make up statements starting with the word "you"; the patient began to feel something as she communicated in this style and a new contact developed between therapist and patient, I once worked with a man whose style was to "spew forth." He over-answered everything. The result was that I frequently did not know what he had said. Seldom looking at me, he would go into his long winded response, his eyes wandering all around the room. To combat this during one session, I leaped from my chair and darted around the room; wherever his eyes went, I went. He had to look at me when he spoke. He became amused and asked me what I was doing. I answered that I wanted to be talked to. What I was doing I explained, was the only way I knew to achieve that. He acquiesced and stated that he could make it easier for me by looking at me when he spoke. I asked him if he was willing to limit his responses to terse statements. He agreed. Feeling structured and awkward at first, he moved into the spirit of the experiment and became amazingly lively. This experience was the lubricant for moving us to our contact boundaries.

The experience of no difference, the lack of uniqueness, or no contact is known in Gestalt therapy as confluence. In confluent relationships, the boundary disturbance is one of sameness; the persons involved agree to not disagree. Confluence is used by people to reduce differences. No sense of boundary exists. Confluent people see to it that nothing new happens; yet at the same time little that is interesting or exciting happens in their relationships. Staleness and drabness are the order of the day. As Perls, et al. (1951, p. 527) stated, "The patient sees to it that nothing new will occur, but in the old there is no interest or discrimination." Confluence results in hanging on to relationships that no longer nourishes. What is impeded is contact (Perls, et al., 1951).

Guilt and resentment clue the therapist to a disturbed confluent relationship. If Larry and Linda are in a confluent relationship and the confluence is interrupted by Larry, he may feel guilty and attempt to restore the confluence by making restitution. If, on the other hand, Larry believes Linda guilty, he will feel resentful; perhaps demanding that Linda feel guilty, apologize, or accept some punishment. What is needed is actual contact. They need to learn to accept and appreciate their differences.

Confluence has its productive forms, as well. Healthy confluence may be the basis for people rallying around a cause, be it political, religious, social, even athletic. Confluence may also be the mechanism behind empathy. When not pathological, confluence can lead to a feeling of oneness with humankind.

Therapy with confluent people, as with the other disturbances, must lead to contact. Discrimination and differentiation are important and no opportunity should be lost for assisting the patient in distinguishing himself or herself from others. With confluent patients I will frequently point out ways that we are different. This public acknowledgment implies that I accept our differences in a nonjudgmental way. Certain experiments enable confluent patients to discern "I" from "you" in relationships. Questions that demand personalized answers may lead to contact or at least to a sense of self. "What are you doing now?" "What do you want?" "What are you thinking?" These are questions that can lead to self-articulation so that confluence will be replaced by true experiences of differences.

Conclusions

It goes without saying that Gestalt therapists need to be aware of their own boundary disturbances. Ideally, through our own therapy and training we dissolve or resolve most boundary difficulties. If we know, for example, that we retroflect, we need to be keenly aware of our tendency when working with retroflective patients so that we do not end up being two people talking to ourselves in the other's presence. Some of us know that with certain types of clients, or in certain situations, we may be interfering with contact. To me, it seems imperative that we be aware of our boundary disturbances and, in situations where they are likely to emerge, ask for supervision.

A colleague, sitting in as supervisor with me and my patient, can often help me to become aware of my own blind spots, of the possibility that I am projecting and do not know it, that I have been grappling with my own conflicts. To establish a contactful, working relationship with that client I would need to work through my boundary disturbance so that I can experience him or her at the contact boundary, rather than interfere in some way with contact. This contact can develop if and when we allow our energy to take us to the contact boundary where we can truly assimilate or reject that which is "not me."

References

Harman, R. (1974). Goals of Gestalt therapy. *Professional Psychology*, 5, 178-185.

Latner, J. (1973). *The Gestalt therapy book*. New York: The Julian Press.

Perls, F. (1947). *Ego, hunger, and aggression*. NY: Vintage Books.

Perls, F., Hefferline, R., Goodman, P. (1977). *Gestalt therapy: Excitement and growth in the human personality*. NY: Bantam Books, (originally published 1951).

Polster, E. & Polster, M. (1973). *Gestalt therapy integrated: Contours of theory and practice*. New York: Bruner/Mazel.

Gestalt Therapy Supervision[*]

Although an increasingly large amount of professional literature has accompanied the growth of Gestalt therapy, very little has been written about the supervision and training of Gestalt therapists. Recent books by Feder and Ronall (1980) and Marcus (1979) are examples of new directions in Gestalt therapy. Greenberg (1979, 1980, & 1981) has published interesting research findings documenting Gestalt therapy's effectiveness. Since 1978 we have had our own publication, *The Gestalt Journal.* In spite of the burgeoning of publications about Gestalt therapy, little has been written about the supervision of Gestalt trainees or the supervision of trained therapists. Our goal in this paper is to describe some of the dynamics of therapist/patient problems and styles of supervision which we have encountered or used.

Supervision ought to be an integral part of any psychotherapy training program. Through supervision, trainees hone their skills and zero in on the artistry of psychotherapy. Typically, supervision consists of a trainee, usually a graduate student, meeting with a supervisor,

---

[*] This article originally appeared in *The Gestalt Journal,* Vol. VI, #1

usually a person possessing the highest degree in his or her profession. These supervisory meetings would be scheduled weekly and would involve discussion of the supervisee's cases, sometimes centering on a particularly difficult case or on more general problems the trainee was having. These supervisory sessions could also include critiques of audio or video tapes. Assessing the accuracy of trainee's diagnoses, preparing a treatment plan, and giving suggestions about what to do are typical topics in traditional psychotherapy supervision. Naturally, the content and style of supervision differs depending on many factors; for example, the theoretical orientation of the supervisor, the experience of the trainee, the needs of the agency, and so on. Some supervisors may, at times, focus on the psychodynamic process of the supervisory session.

Gestalt therapy supervision may include all of the above methods, or may differ quite dramatically in content, purpose and style from the typical supervision described above. The rest of this paper will be devoted to specific kinds of Gestalt therapy supervision.

Dynamics of Therapist/Patient Problems

Gestalt therapy supervision often focuses on the therapist's responsibility for therapist/patient problems. One way therapists contribute to these problems is by refusing to be grounded in Gestalt therapy theory. Poorly trained Gestalt therapists have problems with patients just as poorly trained therapists of any theoretical persuasion do. We have heard "therapists" say, "I tried Gestalt with a psychotic and it didn't work," or some equally uninformed statement that is a giveaway of their lack of understanding of Gestalt therapy theory.

Gestalt therapy is not a "bag of tricks," an entity that can be taken out of a drawer and used or applied; it is a way of viewing people and their problems that springs from a strong theoretical base. Poorly trained therapists do not know this and frequently are incompetent with their patients. They then blame their difficulty on Gestalt therapy and ignore their own incompetence.

Rigid and or inflexible therapists frequently have difficult times with their patients, especially if these patients possess similar character traits. Believing that there is only one way to do therapy frequently will lead the therapist and patient to an impasse that is not dissolved. We must teach our trainees to be flexible, so that if one way of doing therapy does not work they will try something another way.

Teaching a process orientation (an awareness of both our own process and that of the therapy) enables trainees to become more flexible. As they become aware of their unwillingness to try something else, then they can either experiment by trying something else or they can reveal to their patients their own unwillingness to experiment. Acknowledging our stuckness or rigidity to patients will often get one or both of us moving again.

Boundary disturbances on the part of the therapist may be the root of problems in therapy. It is interesting to consider "difficult" patients as projections on the part of the trainee or therapist. That is, the patient possesses some trait or characteristic very similar to the therapist, which the therapist has disowned or is unaware of. In one sense then, the therapist is responding to something disliked in his or her own personality. Trainees may report not liking a particular patient or may report feeling stuck and unable to "understand" their patient. If the therapist has traits and characteristics similar to the patient, there may be a time in therapy when there is no movement at all; both appear firmly entrenched in their positions and unwilling to change. One way to work with projection in supervision is to ask the trainee to "be the patient." One trainee was surprised at the ease with which she became her patient and spontaneously recognized what she was doing as a projection. Asking the trainee to "be the patient" is not only useful with therapists who are projecting, it illustrates other dynamics as well. A male trainee was amazed at his own dullness and lack of interest as he "became" his patient; he discovered how he had mentally resigned, believing he was powerless to do anything with his patient.

Retroflection is another boundary disturbance that interferes with a therapist's effectiveness with patients. Trainees will have thoughts and feelings that they do not or will not share in the therapy session; that is, trainees talk to themselves instead of to their patients. Naturally, when trainees spend a lot of time talking to themselves, they are not available to their patients. Feelings such as anger or boredom are retroflected instead of being utilized in the therapy. It is no surprise that trainees who retroflect feel out of touch with their patients. Trainees need to develop some balance between self disclosure and self containment, they should not blurt out everything that is going on with them. A favorite saying I have heard from Carl Whitaker applies here, "Be crazy but also be smart" (Whitaker, 1982, p. 371).

Feelings of no difference, sameness, or a lack of boundaries is called confluence. When therapists are confluent with their patients they lose perspective and attend only to how they are similar. Perhaps the therapist shares this similarity with the patient by saying, "I know just how you feel." At any rate, any sense of "what is me and not me" is lost for the therapist. A confluent relationship results in the loss of the creative distance that is necessary for much of Gestalt therapy to occur. At best, confluence can be perceived as empathy. At worst, confluence can lead to the therapist acting as a rescuer and merely offering suggestions or advice. Value differences may lead to patient-therapist difficulty. A female trainee reported she was having a hard time working with a woman who was deciding to stay in a dead marriage because of the financial benefits and then later planning "to take him for all she could." This was contrary to the trainee's life experience; she had left a similar marriage in order to "survive" and establish an identity of her own.

Process of Supervision

Gestalt therapy supervision explores the above dynamics and avoids the sterility of just "talking about" patients by making supervision a "here and now" experience. The kinds of supervision described below are attempts to teach and train therapists in Gestalt therapy and to utilize their natural curiosity. Occurring in many settings, Gestalt therapy supervision described in this paper may be individual supervision of students in a graduate degree program or a Gestalt therapy training program, supervision as part of an agencies' on-going programs, or in numerous other arrangements.

One-to-One Supervision

In Gestalt therapy supervision we are interested in what the patient is like. We want to know, for example, how the patient looks at or avoids the therapist, and the degree of consistency between the verbal content and emotionality of the patient. Knowledge of the patient's behavior in these areas helps us to assess the awareness and contact functions of the patient. Supervisory discussions centered around these issues help the supervisee or trainee think in Gestalt therapy terms. It is not that Gestalt therapists eschew diagnosing or assessing; it is that we are interested in the type of diagnosing and assessing that is consistent with our theory and may lead to therapeutic intervention.

Another focal point in one-to-one supervision is how the trainee behaves as supervision unfolds. Some cases are presented vigorously and enthusiastically; the trainee appearing to relish the prospect of learning more about therapy and working with specific patients. At other times we may find dullness, frustration, boredom, discouragement, and so forth, to be the predominant mood of the trainee. The trainee's awareness would then he explored; "How do you dull yourself with this patient?" Sometimes we discover that the trainee has given up on a particular patient because an experiment had been rejected by the patient or led nowhere. The trainee then becomes convinced that "nothing will work" with his or her patient and loses his or her interest and creativity. The purpose of supervision then becomes the exploration of the trainee's awareness so that he or she can return to the patient with increased vigor.

Asking the trainee to "be the patient" or role-play the patient can produce interesting results. The trainee, at times, may move easily into this experiment, embodying the patient in his or her behavior. When trainees do this easily, we discover a lot of similarity between the trainee and patient, resulting in confluence. Both trainee and patient are purring along, waiting for the other to do something.

Audio and video tapes can be used in supervision to help trainees discover what they are missing, and not paying attention to in therapy. Usually this is some nonverbal behavior of therapist or patient that trainees miss because they are paying too much attention to content. Trainees frequently discover their "helpful" or hostile nature, and so on when reviewing their tapes. They can actually see and hear the frequency of offering solutions for patients' problems. Solution giving is to be avoided most of the time in supervisory sessions too. We want to avoid giving the impression that there is a "best" solution and that, if the trainee will "use" it, he or she will be doing Gestalt therapy. Tapes can be stopped anytime. Questions like, "If you were in the session now, what would you say or do?" or "Do you remember where you were at this point in the session?" can be beneficial. Often, we discover that trainees are "in their heads" constructing some grand strategy instead of paying attention to what is happening in front of them. They thereby succeed in missing the most important part of the session which is what the patient is actually doing.

A disadvantage of one-to-one supervision is that it can become nothing more than a "talking about" session. Supervisory sessions that consist mainly of talking about can be very sterile; both parties leave feeling tired and do not look forward to the next session. Supervisees have told us that in "talking about" sessions they feel overloaded with information and frequently leave confused and lacking clarity.

Supervision in Triads

A popular style of supervision in Gestalt therapy training programs involving large groups of trainees is to group participants into triads. In each triad one person will be the therapist, one will be the patient, and one will be the supervisor/observer. The role of the supervisor in the triads varies from one program to another. In some programs the agreement made is that the supervisor will not interrupt unless the "therapist" asks for help. At the end of the session, the supervisor then offers feedback, observations, and suggestions. A style that seems to us to be more useful is to do away with this agreement to not interrupt. The supervisor can inquire of the therapist anytime. Inquiries about the awareness of the therapist, especially about the process of the session, will help the therapist/trainee tune into important aspects of Gestalt therapy.

If one accepts that the essence of Gestalt therapy is "I thou, here-and-now," the triadic supervisor will need to monitor the amount of "I-ness" available in the therapist. Too frequently, trainees rely on questions and premature experiments and leave themselves totally out of the session. A watchful supervisor can help alleviate this problem by pointing it out to the therapist and proposing ways to remedy the situation. Trainees can turn to the supervisor whenever they feel stuck. It may be that the supervisor has some idea about how the therapist got stuck, even to the point of watching the "stuckness" develop in order to determine what the therapist will do. The supervisor can offer his or her observations to the trainee and may even have some suggestions for moving on. Upon hearing a discussion between supervisor and therapist, the "patient" may want to offer his or her two-cents worth. At other times it is helpful to check with the patient about hunches and other assumptions made by the supervisor.

A drawback in triadic supervision, especially in large work-shops, is that the leader is spread too thin. That is, all three members of the triad are trainees; the Gestalt therapy trainer may circulate to whatever triad that interests him or her, or asks for more supervision. Consequently, some triads may have very little or even none of the "expert" supervision.

Group Supervision

One supervisor meeting with a group of supervisees can be an exciting method of Gestalt therapy supervision. In this style of supervision there is a tripartite emphasis: 1) an emphasis on the cases presented; 2) an emphasis on the intrapersonal dynamics of each supervisee; and 3) an emphasis on the interpersonal or group dynamics. A well trained and experienced Gestalt therapist is needed for this style of Gestalt therapy supervision. To prepare trainees for this difficult role I (Harman) have been supervising the supervision of my advanced trainees.

Another accepted form of Gestalt therapy supervision is for trainees to take turns leading or coleading the training group. When the trainee is leading the group, the Gestalt therapy trainer is present and may offer on-the-spot supervision, may comment about the trainee's style, may inquire about the trainee's awareness, may offer suggestions, or supervise in a myriad of ways.

Coleading with the trainer may give the trainee support in getting over his or her initial stage fright and can give valuable training experience. On the other hand, if the trainee defers to the supervisor, what evolves is a situation where the trainee stays mostly in the background.

In Situ Supervision

An exciting form of Gestalt therapy supervision is for the trainer to actually sit in on the session as the trainee works with the individual patient. We prefer that the supervisor be as active as necessary while sitting in. An agreement not to interrupt or comment until the session is over is stifling and not the best way to supervise. The time to comment or interrupt is when the trainee asks for help, or when the supervisor believes it would be profitable. In keeping with Gestalt therapy theory, if the trainee is not aware or is noncontactful, the supervisor would want to interrupt. The purpose of the interruption is to help the trainee become aware of his or her own process. The supervisory interaction between supervisor and trainee takes place in the presence of the patient.

Patients respond in different ways to *in situ* supervision. They should be informed and their consent obtained before the session. In the agency where we work, patients are informed verbally and in writing that it is standard practice for a supervisor to sit in on a session, and they are asked to sign a statement acknowledging that they have been so informed. In the private training program conducted by the senior author, patients are given a reduced fee when they work with one of the trainees and the patient is informed that it is routine to have a supervisor sitting in on the session. If the patient objects, the reduced fee is waived and they are not seen by a trainee. The point here is that with some patients the willingness to have a supervisor sit in is a sign of growth. In some cases we have noticed a decrease in paranoid thoughts, less defensiveness to disclosing their problems and a general loosening up with people.

Peer Supervision for Trained Therapists

The fact that one has completed a Gestalt therapy training program and engages legitimately in the practice of Gestalt therapy does not do away with the need for supervision. One way to do this is to ask peers to sit in on sessions and provide supervision. We do this with patients we are having some difficulty working with and find it a valuable way to continue our growth and learning as therapists. A peer support group can provide supervision as well as a place for trained therapists to periodically work on issues in their own lives.

References

Feder, B. & Ronall, R. (1980). *Beyond the hot seat: Gestalt approaches to group.* New York: Brunner/Mazel.

Greenberg, L. (1980). The intensive analysis of recurring events from the practice of Gestalt therapy. *Psychotherapy: Theory, Research & Practice,* 17, 143-152.

Greenberg, L. & Rice, L. (1981). The specific effects of a Gestalt intervention. *Psychotherapy: Theory, Research & Practice,* 18, 31-37.

Greenberg, L. & Saran, J. (1981). Encoding and cognitive therapy: Changing what clients attend to. *Psychotherapy: Theory, Research & Practice,* 18, 163-169.

Marcus, E. (1979). *Gestalt therapy and beyond.* Cupertino, Calif,: Meta Publications.

Gestalt Therapy Research [*]

Doing the literature search for this article was an interesting experience for me. I was heartened to discover articles about Gestalt therapy cited in Germany, France, Spain, Yugoslavia, and Great Britain. Many articles are being published now in a variety of journals as well as *The Gestalt Journal.* However, quality research on Gestalt therapy remains fairly sparse.

The situation has improved some since Simkin's 1978 article. Simkin (1978) pointed out that it was not until 1973 that the *Psychological Abstracts* recognized Gestalt therapy as an entity separate from Gestalt psychology. In spite of Gestalt therapy meriting a separate listing, confusion, cross listing, and incorrect listings still persist in the *Psychological Abstracts.* My 1978 article on Gestalt marriage and family therapy was incorrectly listed under Gestalt psychology in the *Psychological Abstracts.*

The research reviewed in this article appears to fall into one of five categories: 1) Effects of Gestalt marathons; 2) an analysis of the

[*] This article originally appeared in *The Gestalt Journal,* Vol. VII, #2

Gloria film; 3) comparing Gestalt therapy to other theoretical orientations; 4) analysis of specific Gestalt therapy techniques; and 5) doctoral dissertations. The rest of this article will be divided into these five categories plus a discussion section.

Gestalt Therapy Marathons

Research in following up the effects of Gestalt weekend marathons and ongoing weekly groups by Guinan and Foulds (1970) suggests that Gestalt-oriented groups foster increased levels of self-actualization in normal growth-seeking college students. Foulds and Hannigan (1976) followed up Gestalt marathon participants six months later and discovered that achieved gains in self-actualization persisted over time. Greenberg, Seeman, and Cassius (1978) studied participants in a forty-five hour marathon experience, in which the therapists worked generally from a Transactional Analysis and Gestalt framework. Using the *Tennessee Self Concept Scale,* the *Semantic Differential,* and the *Bach Helpfulness Scale,* they found significant positive changes on all measures for the treatment groups. A two-week post marathon follow-up with the TSCS showed some shrinkage toward baseline, but with continued significant gains on some of the TSCS variables.

Analysis of the Gloria Films

Ramig and Frey (1974) applied content analysis and cluster analysis to the ideas of Fritz Perls to develop a taxonomy of Gestalt processes and goals. Applying these techniques to the Perls *Gloria* film they found Perls' Gestalt therapy can be defined as a process in which the therapist seeks to skillfully frustrate the client in the here-and-now so as to facilitate organic contact with the environment, self-awareness, and maturation and autonomy. Most Gestalt therapists believed this anyway. It is nice to find some beliefs statistically validated!

Using the 14-category Hill *Counselor Response System*, Hill, Tharnes, and Rardin (1979) analyzed the Gloria films of Rogers, Perls and Ellis. They found that *the System* was able to describe the verbal behavior of the three therapists and was able to detect behavioral differences reflective of their differing theoretical orientations. According to Hill, et al. (1979) Perls used mostly direct guidance, information, interpretation, open questions, minimal encouragers, closed questions, confrontations, approval-reassurance, and non-verbal.

Meara, Shannon, and Pepinsky (1979) analyzed *Three Approaches to Psychotherapy* using data generated from a computer assisted language analysis system. Their analysis indicated that the three therapists were different from one another on four dependent measures of stylistic complexity: 1) Number of sentences; 2) average sentence length; 3) average block length; and 4) average clause depth. Results imply, based on linguistic study, that Gloria's work with Perls led to concerted action.

Although they did not use the *Gloria* film, Tellgen, Frassa and Honiger (1979) had raters analyze video taped Gestalt therapy sessions. Significant correlations were found between the therapists' traits of empathy, positive regard, genuineness, and "being-in-the-now," and the patient traits of concentration, involvement, and experiencing. Sessions that were judged "adequate" were characterized by high rates of genuineness and "being-in-the-now" in therapists, and "being-in-the-now" in clients, and pursuit of an internally perceived goal.

Comparing Gestalt Therapy With Other Approaches

Smith and Glass (1977) "meta-analyzed" nearly 400 controlled evaluations of psychotherapy and counseling. They found, on the average, the typical therapy client to be better off than seventy-five per cent of the untreated individuals. Their analysis included many different kinds of psychotherapy, but there was an inadequate number of studies for them to make firm statements about Gestalt therapy's effectiveness. This points out the absence in the literature of controlled studies involving Gestalt therapy.

In a study of the effects of encounter groups, Lieberman, Yalom, and Miles (1973) compared the effects of ten different kinds of encounter groups, including Gestalt therapy. Among many findings, they found one Gestalt group to be among the lowest in producing positive change and one Gestalt group to he among the highest in producing negative changes. Equivocal findings like these need to be replicated.

The effects of the ABCs of Rational Emotive Therapy and the empty-chair technique of Gestalt therapy on anger reduction were studied by Conoley, et al. (1983). They found both treatments successfully reduced blood pressure and lowered *Feeling Questionnaire* scores significantly more than the control condition. However, they were unable to differentiate between the effectiveness of either treatment.

Petersen and Bradley (1980) hypothesized that counselor's attitudes would be a function of their theoretical orientation and experience, They tested their belief with counselors from a behaviorist, Gestalt, or rational-emotive orientation. Results showed a significant relationship between counselor orientation and theoretical tenets. Level of experience did not contribute to counselor attitude. The research of Brunink and Schroeder (1979) is unique in that they used "expert" psychoanalysts, Gestalt therapists, and Behavior therapists instead of graduate students briefly trained in techniques. A content analysis of audiotapes reveal the therapists from the three modalities were similar in their communication of empathy and dissimilar to the other therapists. The authors went on to say that compared to the other two types, Gestalt therapists provided more direct guidance, less verbal facilitation, less focus on the client, more self-disclosure, greater initiative, and less emotional support. More research of this kind, using expert and trained therapists needs to be done. While not germane to this review, I recommend the reading of the Brunink and Schroeder (1979) article because of the interesting and unsuspected findings about analysts and behaviorists.

Married couples were assigned for treatment to either Gestalt relationship facilitation or to relationship enhancement treatment. Jesse & Guerney (1981) found there were significant gains for participants in both groups on all variables studied. Couples increased positively on marital adjustment, communication, trust and harmony, rate of positive change in the relationship, relationship satisfaction, and ability to handle problems. Relationship enhancement participants achieved greater gains than Gestalt relationship facilitation participants in relationship satisfaction and ability to handle problems.

Sohel (1979) investigated preference for behavioral, analytic, and Gestalt therapy. His results showed that young females, but not young males, significantly preferred behavioral therapy for a specific phobia. Under forced choice conditions the group significantly preferred Gestalt therapy. No differences were found for the relationship or preference given a depressive disorder. In related research, Sobel and O'Brien (1979) found no differences in client expectation for positive counseling results from analytic, behavioral, and Gestalt therapy.

Specific Gestalt Therapy Techniques

If there was an award for outstanding research in Gestalt therapy it should go to Leslie S. Greenberg. Greenberg and his associates(Greenberg, 1980; Greenberg, 1983; Greenberg & Clark, 1979; Greenberg & Dompierre, 1981; Greenberg & Higgins, 1980; Greenberg & Rice, 1981; and Greenberg & Webster, 1982) have published some interesting research in which they have investigated a specific Gestalt therapy technique, the two-chair technique of dealing with splits, conflicts or polarities. In a series of studies Greenberg and his associates (Greenberg & Clarke, 1970; Greenberg & Higgins, 1980; and Greenberg & Rice, 1981) found that the Gestalt two-chair technique led to a greater depth of experiencing than did empathic reflection. Greenberg & Dompierre (1981) substantiated the previous findings on depth of experiencing; they also discovered shifts in awareness, reported conflict resolution, and reported behavior changes were greater following the Gestalt interventions than did empathic reflection of feelings. Preresolution and resolution, phases a patient goes through while experiencing the two-chair technique, led to a softening of the "harsh internal critic" (Greenberg, 1980). This "softening" implied an actual change and integration of polarities. Greenberg's (1983) related research demonstrated that conflict resolution performance in the two-chair dialogue occurs by a process of deeper experiencing of previously rejected aspects of the self (Greenberg & Webster, 1982) studied clients who experienced intrapsychic conflict related to making a decision. In this study, clients who experienced a softening of their "critic" showed greater conflict resolution, less discomfort, greater mood change, and greater goal attainment than clients who did not experience the "softening." The findings of Greenberg and his associates support the contention of Gestalt therapists that we provide an intense experience in many of our sessions.

Doctoral Dissertations

A number of dissertations were reviewed for this article. Many of the dissertations were theoretical in nature, compared to research. For example, Norton (1980) proposed a Gestalt theory of child development. For the most part, I am omitting dissertation research not because of faulty methodology, but because of the lack of trained Gestalt therapists. Usually in doctoral research the student provides two to four training sessions for other doctoral students on some specific Gestalt therapy technique. This should not qualify as Gestalt therapy research. Two notable exceptions are the dissertations of Little (1981) and Stewart (1976).

Little (1981), a trained Gestalt therapist, provided ten weeks of group therapy for parents of problem children. After treatment, parents were more like "normal" parents on scores of rejection, ignoring, overprotective, overindulgence, and extrinsic valuing. Gestalt therapy was effective in altering parenting styles described as dysfunctional. Sex role stereotyping in psychotherapy with women as a function of therapeutic orientation and sex of therapist was the topic of Stewart's (1976) dissertation. She compared differences between psychoanalysts and Gestalt therapists and between male and female therapists of each modality in terms of type of response (approach or avoidance) to specific kinds of statements by the female client — dependency, hostility toward others, hostility toward therapist, sexuality, assertiveness, traditional sex role, non-traditional sex role, and career achievement. Gestalt therapists gave more approach responses overall and specifically in response to traditional sex role, career achievement, assertion, hostility toward others, and dependency statements by clients while psychoanalysts were more likely to give avoidance responses to these types of statements. Gestalt therapists showed significantly more favorable attitudes toward feminism than did psychoanalysts.

Discussion

Fagan and Shepherd (1970, p. 241) commented on the difficulty of doing research in Gestalt therapy "most often hard data are difficult to obtain: The important variables resist quantification; the complexity and multiplicity of variables in therapists, patients, and the interactional process are almost impossible to unravel; and the crudeness and restrictiveness of the measuring devices available cannot adequately reflect the subtlety of the process. However, the fact that the task is difficult does not reduce its importance, and the need for many questions to be asked and answered by the more formal procedure available to researchers." The same statement is just as true today as it was in 1970.

Gestalt therapists are seldom found in academic positions, since they would generally rather do therapy than theorize about it. More typically they are in private practice or in service agencies where research takes a backseat to practice. Most Gestalt therapists are not academicians and most academicians are not adequately trained in the practice of Gestalt therapy. Yet academicians, generally superficially trained at best, are responsible for most of the research in the field. I contend that their knowledge of Gestalt therapy is only peripheral and they consequently are unable to properly measure its intricacies. One way around this problem is for Gestalt therapists and research-minded academicians to join forces, to set up controlled studies under joint supervision.

More research needs to he done similar to that of Brunink & Schroeder (1979) in which experienced, trained Gestalt therapists are utilized. Research in which graduate students are "trained" in a few sessions to do Gestalt therapy really is not much of a contribution. Research in which several therapeutic modalities are compared with each other could be valuable in determining what kinds of patients work best with what kinds of therapies.

I am pessimistic about the contributions of the research reviewed here on the practice of Gestalt therapy. As I view it, the influence of research on practice is negligible. What does seem to influence practicing therapists is to find out something about their own effectiveness. For example, if I participated in a research project and discovered that some specific technique I was using had some kind of negative effect on most of my patients, I would soon give up the technique. Personal involvement seems crucial if we are to be much influenced by research.

Greenberg's research on the use of the two-chair technique has offered valuable insight into the effectiveness of that particular technique. I would like to see similar research done on different Gestalt therapy techniques. For example, what happens when patients become aware? How do patients respond to therapist using self, and so on. What has not been done in Gestalt therapy research presents a challenging and fertile future.

References

Brunink, S. & Schroeder, H. (1979). Verbal therapeutic behavior of expert psychoanalytically oriented, Gestalt, and behavior therapists. *Journal of Consulting and Clinical Psychology,* 47.

Conoley, C., Conoley; J., McConnell, J & Kimzey, C. (1983). The effects of the ABC's of rational emotive therapy and the empty chair technique of Gestalt therapy on anger reduction. *Psychotherapy: Theory, Research and Practice,* 20, 112-117.

Fagan, J. & Sheperd, I. (1970). *Gestalt therapy now.* Palo Alto, CA: Science and Behavior Books.

Foulds, M. & Hannigan, P. (1976). Effects of Gestalt marathon workshops on measured self-actualization: A replication and follow-up study. *Journal of Counseling Psychology,* 23, 60-65.

Greenberg, H. Seeman, J. & Cassius, J. (1978). Personality changes in marathon groups. *Psychotherapy: Theory Research and Practice*, 15, 61-67.

Greenberg, L. (1980). The intensive analysis of recurring events from the practice of Gestalt therapy. *Psychotherapy: Theory, Research and Practice, 17*, 143-152.

Greenberg, L. (1983). Toward a task analysis of conflict resolution in Gestalt therapy. *Psychotherapy: Theory, Research and Practice*, 20, 190-201.

Greenberg, L, & Clarke, K. (1979). Differential effects of the two-chair experiment and empathic reflections at a conflict maker. *Journal of Counseling Psychology*, 26, 1-9.

Greenberg, L. & Dompierre, L. (1981). Specific effects of Gestalt two-chair dialogue on intrapsychic conflict in counseling. *Journal of Counseling Psychology*, 28, 288-295.

Greenberg, L. & Higgins, H. (1980). Effects of two-chair dialogue and focusing on conflict resolution. Journal of Counseling Psychology, 27, 221-225.

Greenberg, L. & Rice, L. (1981). The specific effects of a Gestalt intervention. *Psychotherapy: Theory, Research and Practice*, 18, 31-38.

Greenberg, L. & Webster, M. (1982). Resolving decisional conflict by Gestalt two-chair dialogue: Relating process to outcome. *Journal of Counseling Psychology*, 29, 468-477.

Guinan, J. & Foulds, M. (1970). Marathon groups: Facilitator of personal growth? *Journal of Counseling Psychology*, 17, 145-149.

Hill, C., Tharnes, T & Rardin, D. (1979). Comparison of Rogers, Perls, and Ellis on the Hill Counselor Verbal Response

Category System. *Journal of Counseling Psychology,* 26, 1983-203.

Jessee, R. & Guerney, B. (1981). A comparison of Gestalt and relationship enhancement treatments with married couples. *American Journal of Family Therapy,* 9, 31-41.

Lieberman, M. Yalom, I. & Miles, M. (1973). Encounter groups: First facts. New York: Basic Books.

Little, L. (1981). The impact of Gestalt group psychotherapy on perceptions of children identified as problematic. Unpublished doctoral dissertation, University of Kentucky

Meara, N., Shannon, J. & Pepinsky, H. (1979). Comparison of the stylistic complexity of the language of counselor and client across three theoretical orientations. *Journal of Counseling Psychology,* 26, 181-189.

Norton. R. (1980). Toward a Gestalt theory of early child development. Unpublished doctoral dissertation, California School of Professional Psychology, Fresno.

Peterson, G. & Bradley, R. (1980). Counselor orientation and theoretical attitudes toward counseling: Historical perspective and new data. *Journal of Counseling Psychology,* 17, 554-560.

Ramig, H. & Frey, D. (1974). A taxonomic approach to the Gestalt theory of Perls. *Journal of Counseling Psychology.* 1, 179-184.

Simkin, J. (1978) Gestalt therapy and the Psychological Abstracts. *American Psychologist,* 33, 705-706.

Smith, M.& Glass, G (1977). Meta-analysis of psychotherapy outcome studies. *American Psychologist,* 32, 752-760.

Sobel, H. (1979). Preference for behavioral, analytical and Gestalt psychotherapy. British Journal of Medical Psychology, 52, 263-269.

Sobel, H. & O'Brien, B. (1979). Expectations for counseling success. *Journal of Counseling Psychology*, 26, 462-464.

Stewart, E. (1976). A study of sex-role stereotyping in psychotherapy with women as a function of therapeutic orientation and sex of therapist. Unpublished doctoral dissertation, California School of Professional Psychology Los Angeles.

Tellgen, E., Frassa, M. & Honiger, S. (1979). Characteristics of therapists and client behavior in Gestalt therapy sessions. Zeitschrift fur Klinische Psychologie Forschung und Praxis, 8, 148-155.

A Case Presentation in Gestalt Therapy *

Robert Harman — Presenter

Rudolph Bauer
Harvey Freedman
Laura Perls
    — Respondents

Jack Aylward — Moderator

The final event at The Gestalt Journal's *Seventh Annual
Conference on the Theory and Practice of Gestalt Therapy
held May 17th, 18th, and 19th, 1985, in Provincetown,
Massachusetts, was a case presentation in Gestalt therapy.
A transcription of the presentation and responses was edited
for publication here.*

AYLWARD: I'd like to begin by introducing our presenter, Robert
Harman. I'm sure those of you who have been attending our conferences will recognize Bob. He holds a doctorate from the University of

* This article originally appeared in *The Gestalt Journal*, Vol. IX, #1

Nebraska in Lincoln and has been practicing Gestalt therapy for about twelve years. Currently, he is in private practice and is the director of the Counseling Center for the University of Central Florida in Orlando. Before that, Bob was at the University of Kentucky at Lexington and, while there, founded the Gestalt Institute of Kentucky. Most of his training in Gestalt therapy was with Jim Simkin. He completed Jim's three-hundred hour training program. Bob has also been active in workshops and symposia and his articles have appeared in *The Gestalt Journal*, focusing on such topics as contact boundaries, impotent males, marriage and family, research and supervision issues. In addition, he has authored many articles on Gestalt therapy that have appeared in a variety of professional journals.

Now I'd like to introduce our panelists. First we have Harvey Freedman, a psychiatrist from Toronto. Harvey has a diploma in psychiatry and is a fellow in the Royal College of Physicians and Surgeons. He is currently an associate professor in the Department of Psychiatry at the University of Toronto. In addition to maintaining a private practice, he also serves as consultant to the Metropolitan Children's Aid Society in Toronto, the Jewish Family and Child Service, Central Toronto Youth Services, Counseling Services for the Province of Ontario, and as a faculty member at the Gestalt Institute of Tokyo. Most of his Gestalt training was done with Frederick Perls between 1965 and 1970. He was the founder of the Gestalt Institute of Toronto.

Those of you who were here for our last case presentation recognize Rudolph Bauer, last year's presenter. Rudy holds a Ph.D. in clinical psychology and is a diplomate in clinical psychology of the American Board of Professional Psychology. Presently, he is the director of the Psychotherapy Training Center in Washington, D.C. and is on the clinical faculty of the University of Maryland Medical School. He was trained at The Gestalt Training Center — San Diego with Erving and Miriam Polster. He has published numerous articles on hypnosis, object relations theory, and Gestalt therapy.

Next is Laura Perls. Laura, as you know, is one of the founders of the New York Institute for Gestalt Therapy, which began in 1952 after the publication of *Gestalt Therapy: Excitement and Growth in the Human Personality*. Prior to involvement in Gestalt therapy, she was active in Gestalt psychology and completed her doctorate in 1932 on visual perception involving color contrast and constancy from a Gestalt psychology perspective. We will begin by having Bob present his case.

HARMAN: I'd like to tell you a little bit more about my background. I think that may help in understanding how I practice Gestalt therapy. I was born in a farm house in rural Missouri in the same bedroom in which my father and older brother were delivered, by the same country doctor and the same midwife who delivered all three of us. I grew up in a warm, supporting network of grandparents and other adults who always seemed to be available to a boy in time of need. I was somewhat surprised when I went away to college to find that the rest of the world didn't know who I was and didn't care. When you grow up in a town with a population of 218, every place you go people will offer you a drink of water or a cookie. When I went away to the big city, which for me was Jefferson City, Missouri, population 25,000, no one knew who I was. My father was a gentleman farmer and was drafted, not by the military but by the school system. When the war started he was one of the few men around that part of the country with a college education, and it was then that he discovered his love which was coaching basketball and teaching kids, at which he was good.

This is my second career. My first career was in sports and I originally went to college on a basketball scholarship and coached for three years. I liked it, but gave it up when I counted one night that for twenty-two nights in a row I hadn't been home to put my kid to bed. I decided at that point that wasn't the lifestyle that I wanted to live. Now I'm out twenty-two nights in a row doing private practice, but it doesn't seem to matter.

In the early 1970s (and some of you who work in universities and other agencies might remember this) we sometimes had a surplus of funds we'd received from one agency or another. One day my boss came to me and said, "Bob, we've got some money that if we don't spend we'll have to give back, and we'll never get it again." So I hurriedly looked through some mailings that I'd saved and I saw that Erving Polster was giving a workshop in Cincinnati. I lived in Lexington, Kentucky, which isn't far, so I went. I don't think I opened my mouth there although I was spellbound by what I saw happening. I decided, "This is for me!" Shortly thereafter I saw an ad in the *APA Monitor* by this guy named Jim Simkin of whom I had not heard and didn't know. Without consulting my family or my wife, I sent in my deposit. I wrote him the next day and said, "Oh, if you don't find me qualified do I get my deposit back?" Jim took me and so I did most of my training with him. I think that's enough history.

When Joe Wysong called and invited me to present this year's case, I had several thoughts. It would be nice to present a case in which everything worked perfectly, all of my interventions brilliant, and the client cured. That would be a nice ego-trip. Some people who know me tell me that I don't need ego trips, so I decided instead to select a case with which I'm struggling today. I'm currently seeing a female client whom I've been seeing for about eighteen months. I will probably continue to see her for at least another six months. Some of the work has been good; some of it bad. Some things have worked and some things have fallen flat. I have divided the presentation into three portions. In the first part I'll acquaint you with the case. Her name is Rose and I could title this, "The Case of Rose; or, Will She Fit in a Toyota?" I hope to give you the essence of what it was like for me sitting across from her during therapy. I'm then going to describe some of the therapy; and, finally, we'll talk about the case from some theoretical perspectives.

I asked Rose if it would be O.K. for me to present her here and she said, "Yes." I also asked her to write something for me to include here and she readily agreed to do it and never delivered the material. I saw her last week and she apologetically said that she had written material but had misplaced it. She does know that we're talking about her this morning and it's O.K. with her.

I'm not the first therapist Rose has seen. Before moving to Florida she had worked in some mental health centers in West Virginia and Indiana but, according to her report, had not stayed with anyone very long. Rose was thirty-six when I met her. She is now thirty-eight. She heard me speak at the University of Central Florida in "Careers in Psychology"; a mandatory class that every psychology major must take. She then came for an appointment. She had forgotten my name and was assigned to someone else on the Counseling Center staff. Rose, who calls herself "non-assertive," assertively and apologetically asked to be switched to the guy who had come to talk to her "Careers in Psych" class. And so the receptionist went down the row and said, "Hey, who talked to a 'Careers' class?" I acknowledged that it was me and I took her as a client. That was my first contact with her.

She has seen me regularly now for eighteen months with an eight-week sabbatical when she asked my permission not to come. She wanted to go to a women's group about which she had heard. I told her, "You don't need my permission. Do what you think is best for yourself." So, she didn't come for eight weeks and went to this group.

When I first started working with her she told me she was seventy-five pounds overweight. I would have guessed a hundred to a hundred and fifty. My estimate of her weight was that she probably weighed 250 to 275 pounds.

Some of her history: Rose started college out of high school and completed her freshman year and then married. She was married at nineteen and divorced five years later. About six months before she came for therapy, she had ended a relationship with a male with whom she had lived for two years. This was when she began to put on weight. She claimed she gained all of her weight in the span of a year.

Although not revealed to me until later in her therapy, she had a sexually incestuous relationship with her father from age thirteen to age fifteen. He had forced her to comply with his sexual wishes for two years. She was, of course, tremendously guilty, resentful and angry about this and we later explored this extensively.

In our initial encounter in my office I said to Rose, "Rose what do you want?"

She responded that she wanted to work on "her depression and some unresolved issues with her mother." Because I didn't know her well I didn't comment that she sounded somewhat rehearsed to me. During our first session I was struck by two very unusual pieces of nonverbal behavior that she exhibited. Try to remember this: when I spoke she pushed back in her chair as far as she could go, opened her eyes as wide as possible, and held her breath. So, this is what I saw — this huge woman pushed back in her chair with her eyes open as wide as they could possibly go and her chest inflated as far as it could possibly go. As I spoke she maintained this awkward position while exhaling with such force I could feel it across the room. I thought this would be something fine with which to work and so my first comment was, "Are you aware of your expression?"

"No"

"Well, would you be willing to stay as you are and focus your awareness on your face?"

"Yes." Nothing.

So, "Well, Rose, what do you experience with your face?"

"Well, I can feel my eyes open."

"Well, to me you look terrified or terror-stricken;"

Her response was, "That's interesting," which I later reframed to mean, "That doesn't mean shit to me, Bob."

Almost everything I did with her nonverbal behavior fell flat. She complied with every request I made (I'm going to say more about her compliant behavior later) and she got nothing from it.

Later, I experimented with her blowing and said things to her like, "Are you trying to blow me over?"

"No." And that simply got nowhere. That kind of work on my part has continued to go that way for eighteen months. So I naturally tried a few other things along the way.

I did notice what I describe as her overinflated chest. Keep in mind she is a large woman and she told me that before she gained weight that she had large breasts and that men frequently focused their attention on them. She inflated herself in such a way that it exaggerated the appearance of her breasts and they seemed to be presented to me, as I described them to her at one point.

In working with her expressivity, I mimed her. I said, "Look at me when I do what you're doing and see what this looks like for you." I put myself into the same position and tried to get that expression the way she did and it meant nothing to her. I held a hand mirror up in front of her and said, "Look at yourself. What do you look like here?" That meant very little. I asked her to exaggerate, and she complied and attempted to exaggerate and that meant very little to her.

I'd like to add that in spite of her size and this kind of behavior she looked fragile to me. I can not define what particularly looked fragile because she certainly is big, but her expression and the way she moved looked fragile. That's what the appearance of her was like when she sat across from me. So try to visualize that you are working with this large woman who is pushed back (this is early in our therapy), who looks terrified, and who does strange things with her breathing and holds her chest out.

Rose is very much into controlling herself. She tried desperately not to express any feelings, especially feelings of tenderness or anger. Once or twice she felt a little sexy in the sessions and was very embarrassed by that. She tried to control her tears at all times and said things to me like, "I bet you get tired of me coming in here and losing it"; and then not hear me when I replied, "No, I don't get tired of you coming in here and losing it. I get tired of you coming in here and not hearing me." And she did not hear that very well, especially early in therapy. She does hear me some now.

As you might imagine, she brought with her tremendous feelings of guilt, anger, and resentment toward her father. She said things like, "I should have stopped him sooner. I am the guilty party in this": And she was angry at her mother. Her mother should have known that this was going on. Her mother should have put a stop to it. She was angry at me at times for being male. She was very, very self-critical of herself for many things, including the incestuous relationship with her father. She somehow blamed herself for what happened between her and her father. It was difficult work, and I think we worked through that some to a point where she no longer feels that way. Some of her anger was directed outward toward her mother, and we worked through that.

Now, in spite of all this anger (which also included her brother, who was in and out of the house while this incest was going on and claimed to not know about it), Rose saw her role as holding the family together when I first started working with her. In some ways she had become the family mother. Her parents were divorced and had been for many years. Her mother lived in Indiana, her father lived about fifty miles from Orlando, Florida, and her brother lived in West Virginia.

Rose came in some times extremely stressed after having been on the phone for hours the night before listening to her mother complain about not having money, about her illness, about this and about that. Rose called her brother who was closer but he did nothing. Sometimes she came for her session after a trip to her father's to do something to rescue him out of some financial difficulty or some other kind of trouble. So she appeared to have taken on the role of the family rescuer and was very stressed by all this behavior. She literally was spending hours on the phone with her hypocondriacal mother. The picture I had of her mother was of a sickly, old, semi-invalid woman who could barely take care of herself, Imagine my surprise one day when Rose said her mother walked into town every day, three miles, worked eight hours in a garment factory, and then walked home again. And here was Rose, trying to take care of the woman! Her father lived nearby and sometimes had work and sometimes didn't, had remarried, and had a fourteen-year-old son about whom we're going to talk about later.

The early months of working with Rose seemed difficult to me and in my supervision of myself I said things like, "Bob, you're working too hard. You're trying too hard. Perhaps you're expecting too much. Lay back a little. Relax." When I did little nothing happened; when I tried nothing much happened either, so I finally looked for some kind of happy medium. I felt frustrated in her lack of interest in developing her awareness. Sometimes Rose asked me, "What's it like?" or "How do you like working with me?"

I said things like, "Well, it's somewhat frustrating to me, Rose, because you don't appear to be interested in your own experience or your own awareness"; and then she felt criticized.

Rose frequently felt caught when I gave her an observation. Once she said something about having spent a lot of time on the weekend over at her father's. I said something like, "So you're still taking care of your father."

To her that was a very critical comment on my part and she said something like, "You got me again." She usually said something that indicated that she felt criticized and caught by my comments. My hunch is that since she was self-critical she was projecting her criticism onto me and imagining I was doing it to her.

One other thing I forgot to mention earlier was Rose's voice. She spoke as if her voice came from way up here in her throat. After experimenting with her voice a couple of times and getting nowhere, I asked her if she could teach me how to talk like that. (You might want to try this as I describe it to you.) First of all, you have to take a deep breath. And then hold in your air and speak without exhaling. That's how Rose talked to me most of the time — and that's not easy. This explains some of her overinflated chest. It was a strain for her to get her voice out. When we did that experiment, it was the first time that Rose ever laughed in our sessions. After she taught me and I spoke in her manner, I said, "Rose, I would prefer having Willie Nelson as my vocal teacher." She knew who Willie Nelson was and thought that was nice and gave me a little smile. I think she gave it grudgingly.

Gradually, after six months or so, she had loosened a little bit and felt a little more secure and trusting with me. She seemed responsive to my warmth, my humor, my persistence, and my presence. She referred a friend to me who was a fellow student, and she described me to the friend as warm and unrelenting. She seemed most responsive to what Gary Yontef calls the dialogic aspects of Gestalt therapy and she liked what she called my zingers, which I didn't really feel were very zingy. One time we worked on her hurt. She was hurt deeply by the relationship with her father, by her relationship with her ex-husband, and her ex-lover. As she described them my hunch was that they all fit in the same mold. They were not physically abusive to her. They didn't beat her. They were verbally abusive, non-feeling men. We were working on this one day and I said something like, "So you've been used and abused by men and now you are a wounded woman."

This opened a floodgate of tears for Rose and she had the first emotional explosion that she'd ever had in my office. She cried uncontrollably and I offered to hold her, which she refused. I offered to comfort her in some way and she held up her hands as if saying, "Keep your distance!" Nevertheless, I believe that in this session there was some genuine opening and expression and some finishing of this pain. It appeared to me that her breathing was becoming a little more fluid and this helped her generate more self-support. After she had finished this strong emotional outpouring, she said something to me like, "All men are shits."

I responded, "Hmm, I'm a man. Where do I fit into that model?"

She refused to respond other than to say, "You don't": I believe that at this point she began to acknowledge me as a real person and not as someone who had some need to take advantage of her or to use her in some way.

During the first year of therapy she dreaded coming to our sessions and frequently would describe to me how she was thinking of calling to cancel. Her style of coming for our sessions was to come from work instead of coming from class. She worked part time then, and she worked next to a Convenient Food Store. She'd go from work to the Convenient Store and buy a package of Pepperidge Farm cookies and would eat all of them on the ten minute drive from work to my office. So she filled up as much as she could on the way to our sessions.

Her description of me at another time was that I demanded to be acknowledged as a person. "You demand to be acknowledged as a person." I didn't know I was quite that strong although I did feel persistent in being there.

I experimented with her need to fill up. I don't know if there was any connection, but in the sessions she had a very difficult time with silence and wanted to fill up our periods of silence with something. She blushed. She did not allow herself to be withdrawn and to simply be aware of where she went. She started talking about anything and tried to fill up our silence just as she tried to fill up herself most of the time. She ate enormous quantities of junk food, not only Pepperidge Farm cookies (if you come from the mountains, you know what an Old Moon Pie is), and Ding Dongs, and things of that kind. She typically washed them down with a giant sized Pepsi. So she took in enormous amounts of calories just going from one place to another. I asked her about this one time and she said, "Well, there are times when I just have to put something sweet into my mouth." I don't miss too many opportunities to work with things in a session, so I asked her if she could reverse that and she did what I call "went brain damaged on me" and played dumb. I refused to rescue her, and she fumbled around and finally said, "Oh, you mean could I let something sweet out of my mouth?"

I said, "Sure, that's what I was thinking of. Could you say something sweet to me?"

She said, "No."

I said, "Well, does letting anything sweet out of your mouth have any meaning to you?"

She described for me how as a girl she had sung in the choir at church. That had been very important for her and she looked forward to choir practice and singing. I still hadn't learned my lesson yet so I encouraged her, "Perhaps you could do something like that now." She declared her intention to do that — and didn't. I remember Jim Simkin saying to me once, "A declaration of intention is a declaration of intention is a declaration of intention."

Since then, she has said two or three times, "Oh by the way I haven't done anything about singing yet." And I have said, "Good." Rose is childless and had an abortion during her first marriage. She became pregnant and didn't feel up to mothering at that point. She thought her husband was going to leave her, which he did, so she had an abortion. Now she's thirty-eight and desperately wants to mother.

This is part of her pattern, mothering other people. We were working on that in a session and she felt helpless so I asked her to mother herself. This she did somewhat successfully. I thought I was taking a risk, that she would probably refuse me, but I asked her to mother me. I said, "Rose, could you mother me some." This was the first time she reached out for me. She took my hand and patted my hand, consoled me (this just happened in the last six weeks), and reassured me that "things would turn out O. K. for you." I felt moved by that and wept gently and accepted her mothering. Later she told me that she had heard some waiting room gossip that I was having some personal difficulties, as she called them, and that I looked pained, which was probably true. This was one of the first times I felt her responsiveness to me and her reaching out to me.

That's the only time we have touched. I've asked her about that, and Rose's statement is, "I prefer not to."

Rose reported that she was not bothered by my crying during that session, and I believe as she mothered me that she was the most authentic that she has been with me. Part of that scared her. As she reached out to me and mothered me, she reported becoming aware of her nipples, and this scared her. She also had what she called some sexual feelings and this scared her. She does not appear to have withdrawn from me but if I reach out to take her hand when she's hurting she'll withdraw it. I told her that I felt nourished by her that day, and that brought tears to her eyes and no verbal response. Now I don't think this was the sole cause of her sexual feelings, but she does seem to have experienced a reawakening. She's starting to talk about men and about dating and about developing relationships again.

I want to tell you a little bit about one of her dating episodes. In her efforts to rescue and to take care of the family when her father was in financial difficulty, she agreed to take in her fourteen-year-old half-brother. As it turned out, he was a thief in the neighborhood and probably a schizophrenic. When he was in junior high school, Eric went out for wrestling. He discovered that his wrestling coach was a single male in his late thirties and thought the coach might be a good match for his Aunt Rose. Eric came home one day and told Rose that he'd told his coach about her and that the coach wanted to know if he could call her. This scared Rose and she worked on this in a session and finally said "O.K." So the coach called for a date and Rose said, "I can't talk right now, call me back later"; and came in for an emergency session saying, "What do I do, Bob?"

I said, "What do you mean, 'what do I do?' "

She said, "I'm afraid he'll take one look at me and run."

I said, "How come?"

"Because of my weight."

I encouraged her to follow through with this date saying, "Rose, what's the worst thing you can imagine happening?" Her worst fear was that he would turn tail and run when he saw her. And I, having a somewhat perverse sense of humor, began to fantasize about things much worse than that. The worst thing that I could think of was that she might vomit on the table at the restaurant. She thought that was extremely funny. She said, "I chuckled all the way home." When he called that night, she said, "Well, there's something I need to tell you first."

And the coach said, "What?"

"Well, I'm a little overweight?'

And the coach said, "Well, so what?"

"Well, I'm a lot overweight."

Finally the coach said, "Well how much overweight are you?"

And she said, "An awful lot."

And the coach responded, "Well, for Christ sake, will you fit in a Toyota?" She assured him that maybe with a little pushing and arranging that she would fit in a Toyota. The coach came and she did in fact fit in a Toyota Corolla and she had an enjoyable evening.

I asked out of voyeuristic needs, "Did he kiss you good night?"

She didn't want to talk about that, but did say, "I had a good time. We enjoyed our meal. And we may go out again." They haven't, but I know he has called her and they have spoken on the phone a few times. I've forgotten to tell you that Rose has a B.A. in psychology, which she just got the other day, with a minor in art. That's a part of Rose about which I know very little. She has told me that she teaches art to old folks part time at an Orlando art center. This part of Rose is seldom foreground for me, nor does she herself present it. At one time she did tell me that her art teacher was critical of her because her work was not very expressive. He had known some of her work earlier and she seemed to be holding back from her art work.

When Rose came in to tell me about what the coach had said about fitting in the Toyota, she said, "This is the first session that I've looked forward to coming to because I know with your sick sense of humor you'll like this."

She continues to declare her intentions to lose weight. One of the advantages of working in a university setting — this is something that I like and gives me a great deal of gratification — is that I go to graduation, I talk to people whom I know are graduating and I meet their families. Sometimes the students are a little bit embarrassed about telling the families who I am and I usually describe myself as "I'm a friend of your daughter's or son's" or simply say, "I work here."

Rose and I had another emergency session about her graduation. Nowadays you don't have to go through the ceremony; they'll mail your diploma to you. She was torn, "Should I go through this ceremony or not?" This degree was something she had started at nineteen and is now going to finish at thirty-eight so I thought it was important to go through the ceremony as I imagined it would give her some closure and some finishing. I also thought it might possibly be a developmental phase where she would be going into adulthood. At any rate, she told me, "I don't think I can do it because I cannot invite my mother and not invite my father, cannot invite my father and not invite my mother. They're divorced and they would fight." And I said, "How do you know this?" "Well, I just know it."

Her style was to predict catastrophes and then behave as if they are true and not check them out in any way. I encouraged her to check it out. I said, "Well you could ask your father how he would feel about coming if your mother comes. Or you could ask your mother." She decided to go ahead with the graduation, invited her mother down from Indiana, told her father that she was worried about inviting her and her father said, "Rose, I'm very proud of you graduating. Here's the money to get your mother down here from Indiana." So the father paid the air fare for his ex-wife to come to graduation and they sat together.

I was outside in the hall when the processional came through and Rose, given her size with the extra addition of the graduation gown, was very self conscious about her appearance and looked like she was ready to faint. I said something to her like, "Don't trip when you go up there."

She thanked me for that later and said that was what loosened her up enough so that she could "waddle across the stage" to get her diploma. In the hallway where the graduates march there's some mirrors on each side, and Rose has declared her intentions to go back there a year from now and look in that mirror and not see a blimp looking back at her. I hope that will happen for her too.

She has frequently wished she were thinner. And I shared with her a saying that I picked up in eastern Kentucky, "If you wish in one hand and shit in the other one, which one will fill up first?" Think about that one too.

At this point in her life and in our therapy, she has loosened and she seems more responsive to me. She has become moreassertive and she does not apologize for asking to have an extra appointment or to change an appointment. She has gone from part time secretarial work in the insurance adjusters office to becoming a full-fledged adjuster and currently supervises five people. At times she's terrified by that. She's afraid that someone she's supervising will make a mistake and she'll be held responsible for it. She takes on extra work at the office without knowing how to say no. My hunch is that she does a lot of other people's work for them. But she is working and evidently doing O.K.

She does seem open in our therapy to exploring her "no option" style. She did work on her fear of graduation and her catastrophizing about her date. She does appear open to looking at other options now unless she's severely stressed. At those times there are no options for Rose. She told me the other day, again declaring her intentions, that her goals are to lose seventy-five pounds, to develop a relationship, and to have a family. She wants children desperately. The only time she has ever worked on a dream had to do with the emptiness she feels in her pelvic area. She even gave it color and shape and believed that had to do with her need to conceive and to deliver a baby.

Now I want to talk a little bit about some theoretical aspects of this case. I remember what Bob Resnick said here in 1982. I think I'm paraphrasing him somewhat accurately. Resnick said, "Every Gestalt therapist could stop doing any Gestalt technique that has ever been done and go right on doing Gestalt therapy" (Resnick, 1984). I might add to that, "Every well-trained Gestalt therapist could go on doing Gestalt therapy without techniques." That's basically how I have worked and what has worked successfully with Rose. Time worn Gestalt therapy techniques seem to fall flat with her. I've asked her to fantasize speaking to her mother which she does compliantly and gets nothing from it. I've asked her to speak to me as if I am her father. She does and gets nothing from that. I have done a lot of things like that and have produced very little. What has worked is my presence and my personhood. That we share a similar background has also had some impact. Rose is from the mountains of West Virginia. I'm from the rural area of Missouri. Sometimes she relates to some of my rather earthy expressions.

I emphasize developing the awareness continuum which Rose seems to resist some. Maybe I'm not doing it the right way. But she does seem responsive to me when I'm non-techniquey.

I believe I have expressed myself to Rose regularly, judiciously and with discrimination. I have shared my observations, my preferences, my feelings, and my personal experiences in the sessions with her with regularity. That's what seems to have, over eighteen months, made some difference in her life.

To me, her primary boundary disturbance appears to be retroflection. Her energies and feelings do get stirred up, especially around her family or by some things that I've said to her. Her contact is brief, and I think it's expanded some from when I first started working with her. She would, and still does to some extent, typically interrupt any full engagement, perhaps out of fear of hurting others or of being hurt, and then turn her energies on the only safe object in the field — herself.

Her language has been full of what I call retroflective talking or "splitting talking." She says things like, "I said to myself"; "I made myself"; "I heard myself say." She goes off into what I call a retroflect-ive conversation with herself right in my presence. In my presence she would seem to disappear and go off and appear to be having this nice little conversation with herself. I have focused on that and have asked her in many ways, "Rose, say to me what you just said to yourself. Would you be willing to make that conversation public? Would you be willing to speak to me? Would you come back?" In some ways that seems to have been productive. She likes my doing that.

A secondary boundary disturbance, and most of you know this one is coming, is introjection. That is, she would interrupt herself between awareness and energy mobilization. She becomes aware and then interrupts it somewhat. As an introjector she replaces, it seems to me, her own potential energy and drive with someone else's. Typically, we would describe the introjector as someone who bites off huge chunks, swallows them whole, and doesn't assimilate or digest. That is some of what she does. I thought how this might relate to her eating style, and out of my curiosity, I checked this out with her and got very little from it. It just didn't go anywhere. Part of what Rose describes to me I believe fits with the introjector in that she doesn't have much identity. She felt "identity-less" when we first started working because she had taken in quite a bit from the environment that wasn't her at all. She had a lot of shoulds. I have some questions that to which I hope our panel can respond about the work I've done with Rose. She typically devalues her own experience and awareness, and still does sometimes when stressed. I have struggled with how to work with that. We do what I think is a nice piece of work, and she gets very little from it. Or, if I tell her what I got from it she says, "Oh, yeah, I get that." So I get worried about reinforcing her introjective style.

I think perhaps I'm too impatient. But, after all, I've been working with her for eighteen months.

I work hard with her to help her undo her retroflection, and I've told you some of the things that I say to her such as, "Speak to me directly. Say this to me. Look at me when you say this" — things of that kind. I wonder if I've been too active, too aggressive in working with these. I have experimented with laying back and from my perspective very little happened when I did. I've wondered if that's my impatience, if I'm unwilling to wait.

Rose has never asked me directly to help her lose weight, and I've never tried. I also wonder about that since it's such an obvious problem for her. Should I be more active in encouraging her to lose weight? We have explored that and for her the weight seems like a thick, insular boundary that protects her from the world, particularly men. I quote Rose, "Who would want to go out with a fat lady?" I wonder how the panel and the audience feel about this. Would they be more interested, more aggressive in trying to help her lose weight?

It didn't take me long to catch on to her compliant behavior, that she will do most anything I ask her to do except touching or allowing me to touch her. Most other experiments I propose she will do. Somewhere in the literature, I can't remember who said it, but someone differentiated a cooperative patient from a compliant patient. And I think for quite some time Rose was a compliant patient, doing exactly what I asked her to do and in that way sabotaged our work.

My final concern has to do with people who declare intentions in a session to do something outside of the session. Whenever possible I try to bring that into the session. For example, "I'm going to work on relationships." "O.K., well here we are relating to each other, Rose. Let's work on our relationship." That sends her off into a befuddled fog not knowing what to do and looking to me for instructions. I again feel if I give her too much I will be reinforcing some of her introjects.

She says, "I'm going to be more assertive later."

"Well, Rose. Can you be more assertive with me? Are you getting what you want from me? Could you ask me for something?" And this gets some production from her. She is willing to ask; and once, after spending weeks of screwing up her courage, she accused me of being patronizing. I thought I had been teasing with her and she realized that, but she thought I was patronizing and told me about that. And that was a good lessor, for me to learn.

Finally, I want to mention something about her job. She's totally self-supporting and supports other family members from her salary. She frequently thinks of quitting because she feels stressed and pressured and doesn't have anything else in mind. She graduated in May and university rules do not permit us to work with anyone who is no longer a student. I don't pay much attention to rules so we made a contract that I would continue to work with her through August even though she's not a student. So, I see her at eight in the morning which is fairly early, but she does come and seems to be coming to the place now where she enjoys coming for sessions and is asking more about me, "Now how are you doing, Bob? What's going on with you?" I know she will want to know how this presentation went. She'll be curious about this. If I tell her it didn't go well she'll probably think it was her fault in some way.

AYLWARD: We have something unique to work with here, namely an unfinished case. This is different from what I call workshop therapy or the types of cases you see in textbooks or on film where phobias are cured in twenty minutes or mental health is anchored with the touch of a finger. There seems to be a lot of room for intervention here. Before taking questions from the audience, I'd like to hear a general reaction from each of our panelists. Harvey?

FREEDMAN: Thank you for the opportunity to share my reactions to this very interesting case presentation. Robert, to hear someone present a case that is in midstream, struggling, uncertain, and incomplete is a rare experience. Most of the presentations that I've heard over the years have included startling successes, major break-throughs, or small miracles. So I want to compliment you to start with on having the honesty and the courage to present a case in the way you have.

First, some general remarks. Although Robert has already undertaken the work with this patient, I want to raise the question of whether or not he should have in the first place. I believe that psychotherapy, like many drugs, is over-prescribed by its practitioners, particularly the insight-oriented or awareness therapies. Someone once said that psychotherapy is too good for sick people. Cruel as that jest is, could it apply in the instance of Rose? Should Robert have undertaken psychotherapy with someone who has been so badly damaged? Rose has been very badly damaged. Rose has been very badly nurtured. She had a childlike mother who sought parenting from her daughter, and she had a father who sexually abused her. With this background, is it conceivable that she is a seriously emotionally handicapped person who will remain handicapped in spite of the best-intentioned therapy?

Let me raise some examples from other areas. We know that during certain critical periods in biological development, if the growing infant does not receive adequate Vitamin D, for example, the growth center atrophies, fuses, and rickets are the consequence. Regardless of the amount of Vitamin D given after the biological clock has called it quits, regardless of all further input, those bones will never grow again. Closer to home, we know there are certain critical times for learning and imprinting, that certain things must take place at certain junctures in time for adequate emotional development. Remember how the goslings followed Konrad Lorenz as their mother? Even if the mother who hatched the eggs was presented to these particular goslings after forty-eight hours, it would have been too late for them to unlearn this imprinting. So, with those analogies in mind, has Robert undertaken Gestalt therapy with someone for whom it is too late? Now, I don't know whether this is true or not in this instance; I'm only raising the question for heuristic purposes.

From the point of view of Gestalt therapy, Robert, I believe you're making the error of end-gaining. This is a term which both Laura and Fritz Perls took from F. M. Alexander, who pointed out the distinction between a goal and the means whereby. The means whereby has to do with being focused in the present and paying attention to process, in contrast to expectations which are future-oriented. You say again and again, "Am I too impatient? Am I too aggressive?" May I ask again, are you too ambitious? Is it conceivable that her excess weight is an essential support system to Rose at the present time, and I don't believe that her losing it ought to be the goal of Gestalt therapy.

A few specific comments now. I would like to reinforce something that the patient has already brought to your attention. She described you as "warm and relentless." I find you warm and relentless too, and I think these characteristics are most important in a therapist. So, if she is not psychologically handicapped, and your goals do not have to be limited, then you are in a position to be very useful to her. Growth and learning in Gestalt therapy are considered to take place in that optimum situation between support and frustration, and I believe this is what she's commenting on: you are both supportive, and frustrating, when you need to be.

PERLS: I think your patient was very right when she said that your humor touches her most. It literally tickles her. And that loosens up her breathing — mainly her diaphragm. Sometimes she laughs when you give interpretations which you actually do when you describe something that she hasn't been aware of at all. I would start the other way around, to let her describe what she does and how she does it. It seems obvious to me that . . . I actually made my first note about the promises she gives on the telephone and then doesn't keep, and so on and so on. She bites off more than she can chew and her overweight confirms that she swallows without chewing. She stuffs it in. She drinks her food rather than eating it. I would concentrate with her on the details of how she copes with food as well as how she copes with anything else — with very small things. The client sits as if in the dentist's chair: frightened expression, holding her breath, bracing herself as if expecting pain, thus desensitizing against it. Her emphasis is on holding the inhalation, the blowing out only happens when she can't hold in any longer. So relating the blowing to the therapist doesn't mean anything to her, nor does her own face in the mirror or the feel of it as long as she desensitizes. This also reduces her total energy, so of course her movements look "fragile." In her desensitized state Rose has no support for real interest and full awareness.

I wouldn't give up on her and say she is too damaged. She is full of introjects, and by going too fast you put more into her and it burdens her more. She is holding in so that she actually lets out her breath only when she isn't expressing anything in particular. She just blows off the energy she has which does not go into communication or real expression but is wasted. And I would concentrate with her mostly just on these immediately perceivable and demonstrable attitudes. And stay right in the actual situation.

One does not practice the awareness continuum. The ongoing Gestalt formation takes place when blocks (the fixed behavior gestalten) are dissolved.

You are, as Harvey said, too ambitious and you want to do something or to achieve something with her and in that way you become, in a way, another abuser who just submits her to something that she immediately closes up against and desensitizes. And, of course, the fat helps to desensitize. That's all for the moment.

BAUER: What your presentation raised for me was the ever reoccurring question as to whether I am an agent of change or am I a vehicle for healing. Depending on which of these positions I place myself in, the case — your case — or my own will look rather different. This is especially true when there is a clear symptom — like weight — and is even more true when the patient's story is one in which there is a history of a lot of damage. Often if I conceive of myself as an agent of change the person's stuck point looks quite impossible. The process is very frustrating and I feel that I have to go someplace and the person must grow. If I am able to make that primary shift to a healing position — then whether the person has a presenting symptom or a history of damage makes no difference — because there is no place to go.

In the work you presented here, it seems to me there was a progression and a shift from you being in a position as an agent of change (with the corresponding experience of symptoms, resistance) to the point or place of a healing relationship wherein she begins the process of the self healing the self. Healing — basic healing — comes from within rather than from without; healing as a process includes both the patient and the therapist; the process is greater than the therapist, greater than the patient; the healing process doesn't depend on a person's history, doesn't depend on a symptom — it is more basic than history, more basic than symptom.

AYLWARD: What became exciting for me as you were presenting, Bob, was something that Sonia Nevis has talked about and something I need to be reminded of, namely, how important it is to pay attention to the client's ground in addition to attending to what may be figural at any given time within the therapeutic context. Your involvement with her dating behavior, her trips to the store, her relationships outside of therapy gives a creative balance to your intervention. It's important to note that as we sit in the awe of the existential moment, it's easy to forget that someone has to do the dishes.

Editors' note: A question-and-answer period about a half-hour in length followed Harman's presentation and the panel's responses. A variety of topics were touched on, but none in enough depth to warrant their inclusion here.

– jw

Gestalt Therapy Without Techniques:
A Session with Sue *

As the title of this paper implies, the session presented here is one devoid of popularized Gestalt therapy techniques. The session is exemplary of Resnick's (1984) statement, "Every Gestalt therapist could stop doing any Gestalt technique that has ever done and go right on doing Gestalt therapy." This session highlights the important Gestalt therapy goals of increasing awareness and expanding contact boundaries.

This was my first session with Sue. I had interacted with her socially for a brief period the previous day. Sue reported that she had been in therapy previously. Sue is a tall, athletic looking, thirty-two-year-old woman. One of my first impressions was of how healthy she looked.

I have used a dash (—) to indicate pauses in the session, where I think it necessary I have indicated the length of the pause. My comments are included so that the reader can have some idea of what I think is going on, to comment on some aspect of Gestalt therapy

* This article originally appeared in *The Gestalt Journal*, Vol. X, # 1

theory or application, or to add some information that I think may be helpful.

This session exemplifies my style of working in the present and demonstrates the fertile possibilities of this style. There are places in the session when it would have been easy to get into an explanation, discussion, or to end up talking about. I avoided that most of the time in order to stay focused on the "now."

I don't think I led or pushed Sue at any time during the session. Most of the focus is on what she is doing. I seldom asked her to be or do anything other than what she was doing; the exception is the experiment with her eyes.

Session With Sue

Bob: Hello — I'm imagining that you're cautious and hesitant to start with me this morning.

Sue: I'm thinking that I've usually had a dream, I've had a ticket of admission to work, and I would like to experiment with having a session without having anything specific to work on.

Bob: What is your experience now of having nothing specific?

Sue: Well, I'm looking at you. It looks to me as if you are not looking at me. Are you looking at me?

Bob: Yes, I'm looking at you — so, when you're not specific what happens is that you imagine I'm not looking at you.

Sue: Yes, — you look like you're looking at my left eye.

Bob: I'm moving around Sue; I'm looking at different parts of your face and you.

Sue: Oh, —

Bob: If you would be willing I'd like you to look around, to look at different parts of me.

Comment No. 1: At this point Sue's eyes seemed "locked" on mine. I imagined she was squeezing or forcing herself to look at me and in the process had lost contact with the ground and only my eyes were figural for her. So I requested her to loosen her gaze and to take in more with her vision.

Sue: Okay —(she did some looking).
Bob: What is that like for you?
Sue: I liked doing that. I liked just looking at you.
Bob: I was fantasizing that you were locked on my eyes and paying attention to or noticing anything else.
Sue: Um hmm, when I started looking at you I noticed your lines right here (pointed to her face). I noticed your curly hair (laughed). I noticed the way you're sitting and your socks — (she looked at me expectantly).

Comment No. 2 : We seemed to be trading sentences. This was a pattern I wanted to avoid so I decided to disclose what I was feeling and imagining.

Bob: I'm feeling left dangling. My hunch is that if I don't come in with something I will be left hanging.
Sue: By me?
Bob: By me or by you, I don't know.

Sue: I feel apprehensive and tension sort of holding my arms and planting my feet on the floor. There's a tightness in my chest.

Bob: (I noticed that her chest was barely moving.) Are you breathing?

Sue: A little.

Bob: Would you be willing to do some breathing now? (She breathed deeply several times and I thought I noticed something.) As you exhale I imagine you're shaking your head just slightly.

Sue: Oh (went back to deep breathing).

Bob: What do you notice?

Sue: I notice when I hold myself there is a certain shaking that goes on across the back of my shoulders and back of my neck and it's kind of like this (she shook her head in a jerky, horizontal way). When I breathe and let the air out it's kind of like a shudder across here (points to chest). (She kept on focusing on her breathing.) I feel like I can get air into my abdomen better than I can get it into my chest and shoulder area.

Bob: Is that what you are trying to do, to get air into that part of you?

Sue: Um hmm (she stretched and leaned back in her chair).

Bob: What was that like for you?

Sue: It expanded my chest for me. When I worked with a therapist last summer he mentioned that I looked dead to him from here to here (indicated area of upper chest). And I've been more aware of that area of my body.

Bob: Of looking dead there or what?

Sue: Of feeling numb here, of not breathing into it.

Bob: Do you feel numb there at this moment?

Comment No. 3: I wanted to keep her focused in the "now," that was the purpose of this question. I suspected that it would have been easy to get lost in an explanation of her previous therapy and I wanted to avoid that.

Sue: No, breathing helped at this moment. I became aware that that is the area of my body I seem to deaden most.
Bob: Are you dead there at this moment?
Sue: No.
Bob: What do you experience there at this moment?
Sue: Not as much of a flow there as in the rest of my body.
Bob: You have some kind of blockage there, not as much of a flow?
Sue: Um hmm, I had open heart surgery when I was sixteen and I have a protective feeling about this area of my chest.
Bob: Do you feel protective about this area of your chest at this moment?
Sue: Yea, I feel it is a vulnerable part of my body. I feel vulnerable there.
Bob: What could I do to that part of your body?

Comment No. 4: Again, I wanted to stay with her existential experience. She had just disclosed something very personal to me. What I wanted to stay with were the feelings she had now and what effect this "heart problem" had on her now. I wanted to avoid stories about this. My question tended to focus on our interaction and what impact I might have had on her.

Sue: What could you do — well.

Bob: What I'm in touch with is that you have been remarking about this part of your body the last few minutes and at times you feel dead there; now you feel not flowing, you had open heart surgery and you feel vulnerable. I'm wondering if you have some fantasies about what we might do here. (She started crying.) I'm noticing your tears at this moment.

Sue: I cry a lot, I don't know why. I think it must be tension relief. (She smiled at me while still crying.)

Comment No. 5: What was foreground for me was the split between her eyes and her mouth. Also, I imagined she would have given many reasons for her crying; none of which would have been as productive as staying with her crying and how she experienced her self.

Bob: What I'm paying attention to is your eyes are crying and your mouth is smiling when you told me that.

Sue: (She nodded her head in agreement.)

Bob: Have you any fantasies, Sue, about what I might do, or if I might do something to you here? (I was referring to her chest area.)

Sue: It wouldn't be that you would physically do anything to me there, but that — that's my vulnerable spot. If you see that part of me then you have touched a weak part, a vulnerable part of me and I'm exposed to you and vulnerable to you.

Bob: So you would like for me not to touch your weak part and for you not to be exposed to me. That would make you feel even more vulnerable.

Sue: It is painful to have you touch the part of me I feel is vulnerable.

Bob: How do you know that?

Sue: Because I'm crying right now. I feel vulnerable right now.

Comment No. 6: I imagined this to be a myth and I asked for evidence. Here, I was very aware of her crying and obvious pain. I could have focused my attention on this and decided not to. I was interested in learning something and imagined there was more for her in checking out this "myth"; so I persisted along this line.

Bob: How do you know it is painful for me to touch your weak part?
Sue: — all I know is that just talking about it I cry (sobbing). I don't
    know whether that's painful or not (she contorted her face and
    bit her lip as if to stop crying).
Bob: I'm not experiencing touching your weak part. I'm in touch with
    your crying. I imagine that to be something other than me
    touching you in a vulnerable place.
Sue: — could you be more specific? I mean, could you give me your
    fantasy about why I'm crying?

Comment No. 7: I was not intentionally being evasive. I had no fantasy about why she was crying. Even if I did I doubt if I would have gone into it. We were working well at this point and I didn't want to interrupt out working with a guessing game about why she was crying.

Bob: No, — I wonder what you are in touch with at this moment?
Sue: I feel more alive.
Bob: Maybe I have touched you a little bit there, and don't feel pained,
    you feel more alive right now.
Sue: Right.

Bob: What do you think of that? That doesn't seem to fit your myth. What are you doing now?

Sue: Um —I feel sort of embarrassed now.

Bob: Embarrassed about —

Sue: Crying.

Bob: What I said was that maybe I had touched your weak part and you felt some life there which is contrary to what you predicted. I asked you what you thought about all that, you seemed withdrawn to me and what you tell me is that you are embarrassed about crying.

Sue: — it's true it's not painful. But it is painful, I feel pain in exposing myself to you.

Bob: Where?

Sue: I feel uncomfortable.

Comment No. 8: Sometimes I believe it is important to accurately label what is going on. So I wanted to know precisely where she felt pain. What she discovered was that she was uncomfortable and this seemed to fit.

Bob: I believe that you feel uncomfortable, — you have a squeezed look, you seem to be fearful at this moment, that's my fantasy.

Sue: (She nodded.)

Bob: Is that what you experience?

Sue: No, I don't feel fear.

Bob: What do you feel?

Sue: Um, I feel, I feel myself locking myself into your eyes. I lock myself into your eyes and the rest of the room fades out.

Bob: — Now, when you lock yourself into my eyes what do you experience?

Sue: It is a way of spacing out. I feel, I feel like I lock myself into your eyes and I just sort of space out, I sort of go blank.

Bob: Would you do the opposite of what you are doing now?

Sue: (She looked around, reached for a Kleenex.) When I do the opposite I look around, I look at all of you, not just at your eyes.

Bob: Somehow you have a way of locking yourself in on my eyes, becoming inflexible and not knowing what's out there and feeling spacy. When you allow your eyes to move you start feeling differently.

Sue: Yes, when I allow my eyes to move around I feel just right here.

Bob: If you want to be not right here, then you can lock in on my eyes.

Sue: Um hmm —

Bob: What is happening?

Sue: I was just flashing between locking in on your eyes and not. When I look right at your eyes I start doing that locking.

Bob: You appear to come up in your chair some when you talk about locking in on my eyes.

Sue: (She looked puzzled.) — I was just thinking when you said what could I do to you there (pointed to chest), that set off these tears (started crying), but I don't know why.

Bob: I'm not very interested in your not knowing why. I am interested in how you set your tears off right now. What could I do to you?

Sue: (More crying and shaking of her head.) I have a fantasy of saying you couldn't do anything to me I wouldn't let you do.

Bob: I'm having a different fantasy. What could you do to me?

Sue: What could I do to you? — I just flashed that is your heart and I could hurt you, I mean if you let me I could hurt you in your heart.

Bob: What could be another possibility?

Sue: I could make you feel good.

Bob: Yeah, — seems to me as if you 'lock in' in many ways, you lock in to my eyes and you lock in with one choice and give yourself no others. The only thing you are aware of is "I could hurt you"; there are other possibilities.

Sue: Yes, that's true.

Bob: — What's going on?

Sue: Something a previous therapist said to me just flashed into my mind. One time I said that if I ended the present relationship I was having I would never find another one and he said he didn't believe that.

Bob: What happened, did you end that relationship?

Sue: Yes, and started another one right away.

Bob: Again your myth, what you said to yourself didn't turn out.

Sue: Right.

Bob: So you opened your heart to somebody else?

Sue: It just happened.

Bob: You had nothing to do with it (jokingly).

Sue: It was a surprise.

Bob: I experience you as more open to me at this moment. I feel more open also.

Sue: Yeah, I feel warm toward you right now.

Bob: — I'd like to come back to here (pointed to my chest) and ask you if your warmth is from here to here.

Sue: Yes, I feel air and aliveness there. When I first came in I didn't.

Bob: You look pained again.

Sue: No, — I'm thinking of this relationship I'm starting and during this session I'm seeing myself as an emotional person. I never saw myself as that before.

Bob: Is that OK with you?

Sue: No (tears and shaky voice).

Bob: What's your objection?

Sue: I associate crying with weakness. I want to be composed.

Bob: That's not what you are doing at this moment. With this new person, this new relationship, you want to be non-emotional and composed?

Sue: No, mostly in this therapy session.

Bob: With me you want to be non-emotional and composed?

Sue: Right.

Bob: What could happen? What's happening to you right now? You are emotional, right? (She nodded.) How is that for you?

Sue: I imagine you would see me as emotional.

Bob: I do (she laughed).

Sue: I mean like a silly woman.

Bob: I don't — I'm wondering what your fantasy is of me if I see you as an emotional and a silly woman. You evidently don't want me to see you that way.

Sue: That's right.

Bob: How do you want me to see you?

Sue: I want you to see me as courageous and centered.

Bob: Courageous I know something about, when you say centered I
     don't know much about what you mean.
Sue: Accepting myself, in touch with myself, and calm; relating to you
     non-hysterically.
Bob: I see you as relating to me and emotional and not accepting parts
     of yourself. That's my experience of you so far.
Sue: (Crying.) I wonder where all this sadness comes from. Sometimes
     I just feel like I could cry for days.

Comment No. 9: My hunch here was that she didn't listen to me very
well. When I was talking she had switched to something different. I
could have explored that or waited to see if it happened again. I chose
to wait and stayed with what was going on.

Bob: How long do you feel like you could cry right now?
Sue: I could cry the rest of this session easily (started laughing when I
     looked at my watch).
Bob: That would give you twenty minutes. — Are you sad at this
     moment?
Sue: — No, right now I'm not sad.
Bob: You cried about five seconds (she laughed at this). What's going
     on?
Sue: That just made me laugh, I don't feel sad right now.
Bob: That's the third time I'm aware that you have made a prediction
     about yourself and it hasn't come true.
Sue: — Uh huh, when Cindy said she saw sadness in my, that made
     me feel sad.
Bob: Cindy said this to you in group?

Sue: Yes. I don't know what that sadness is.

Bob: Are you sad at this moment, Sue?

Sue: No, I'm not sad right now.

Bob: What are you.

Sue: I feel relaxed right now.

Bob: Could you make yourself sad?

Sue: Make myself sad? — No, that feels artificial to me. I suppose I could have a fantasy and try.

Bob: You could say to me now you won't feel sad. You are willing to talk about it and you won't feel sad.

Sue: I won't think about something to make myself feel sad.

Bob: Often you seem to make yourself feel sad or puzzled, and don't know why, that's pretty consistent and the implication is that you should know why. What's happening to you when you listen to me?

Sue: It rings true for me.

Bob: What's going on?

Sue: I was just wondering why I do that.

Bob: Are you sad now that you are wondering why you do that?

Sue: No, — tears are funny. When I worked with Cindy yesterday, the fear of working with her I'd gone over beforehand and then the build up of tension I felt the tears coming on. I felt they were related to that, just that, tension.

Bob: You equate your tears with a release of tension for you.

Sue: Yes.

Bob: One way not to be a hysterical woman is to stop tensing yourself.

Sue: (Nodded) Right.

Bob: It was my fantasy that when I said that to you that you begin to tense.

Sue: Yes, yes I did; that's something to think about (laughed).

Bob: I'm noticing you go here (points to chest where she is stroking herself) when you say that's something to think about. Would you do that some more please? — What is that like for you?

Sue: Like soothing myself.

Bob: I am interested in what you're doing. You are talking about thinking and your hand goes here around your heart. That is not where you do your thinking. — What are you aware of doing now?

Sue: Just touching myself here.

Bob: What's happening here now (I indicated the area of her chest where she was touching herself)?

Sue: It makes me bring up sadness.

Bob: It makes you bring up sadness.

Sue: I feel sad, I touch myself here.

Bob: That's different than weakness for me. The sentence that's running through my head is, "I'm relieved to be alive, I still don't believe that I survived that surgery." Would you like to try that on?

Sue: I'm relieved to be alive and I still don't believe that I survived that surgery.

Bob: Would you say that again please?

Sue: I'm relieved to be alive and I still don't believe I survived that surgery (her words flowed easily and seemed synchronized with her breathing).

Bob: What happens to you as you say that to me?

Sue: I experience this feeling of excitement here (pointed to chest).

Bob: As you were saying that I felt fluttery through here, through my chest.

Sue: I've never said that before (cried). That makes me feel joyous to say that. I don't know why.

Bob: What you do know is that you feel joyous.

Sue: Yeah — I feel a co-mingling of joy and sadness about that.

Bob: I don't know about your — about that. I believe you that you feel a co-mingling of joy and sadness.

Sue: Yea, yeah, —

Bob: I'm mostly aware of your face at this moment. You don't look joyous, I imagine there's sadness there.

Sue: I feel joyous from here to here (pointed from eyes to chin) and I feel a heaviness from here upward (eyes to top of head), sort of weighing on my head.

Bob: I imagine that's probably your 'whys' or your 'about thats' (said teasingly). What I am doing is trying to brainwash you into giving up your myths. (Jokingly) You don't want to do that, do you? (Sue laughed) You will want to hold on to your condition, your explanations, your correlations. You look joyful at this moment. (Sue was laughing and looked bright.)

Sue: My chest feels more joyful but from here to here I feel heavy (pointed to above eyes to top of head), mostly in my forehead.

Bob: Give that up and all you'll have left is your heart. — I'd like something from you. What kind of guarantee did they give you? How long is this by-pass, this valve in your heart, supposed to last?

Sue: A lifetime guarantee, they said I'd probably outlast most other people. He said I would never be a ballerina, but I could do any form of physical exercise with moderation, that I would have a slight murmur but there was every reason to believe I would have an average life-span.

Bob: Which in your family is how long?

Sue: Well, my grandfather is ninety (laughter).

Bob: So you're stuck for fifty + years.

Sue: Yes — but, —

Bob: But —

Sue: I was thinking it all feels so fragile to me (softly).

Bob: Say again.

Sue: I feel so fragile.

Bob: How might you break?

Sue: I feel like I've been sort of opened up and then put back together, mended. I'll probably last, but I'm sort of vulnerable at that place. I might break, I'm fragile in that way.

Bob: So your doctors have told you that you will live a normal life-span which in your family could be ninety and you have a feeling of fragileness in this part of you. At this moment do you feel fragile or vulnerable here?

Sue: No, at this moment I don't feel particularly fragile. I think of myself as that way sort of in general.

Bob: Do you believe that, do you believe you see yourself as sort of fragile in general?

Sue: (Laughingly) I see my chest area as fragile. No necessarily the rest of myself.

Bob: Your chest doesn't look very fragile to me. — I was thinking of your job where you work with fifteen preschoolers and imagining what that would be like if you were fragile.

Sue: It would be impossible, no I'm not fragile with them.

Bob: You might experiment with leaving off your "them" and see how that sounds to you.

Sue: I'm not fragile.

Bob: Only when it pays I'm fragile.

Sue: (Sue was laughing.)

Bob: You look very delightful right now.

Sue: It's so true sometimes it does pay to be fragile. No, I'm not fragile. I'm not fragile.

Bob: I believe that. It's you I want to convince! The broken heart myth was one that just wasn't true. Your heart was broken by that brute who left you, and in a few weeks this fragile little thing found another brute.

Sue: This one isn't a brute, he is totally different. He builds harpsichords. He tells me he loves me all the time, that he thinks I'm beautiful.

Bob: How does that make you feel?

Sue: I love it! He sees me as strong, not as fragile, he makes me split the wood.

Bob: (With feigned incredulousness) He makes you split the wood! (Laughed) He doesn't let you get by with being a baby! He doesn't keep you at home, looking at you and keeping you fragile.

Bob: OK, I notice that our time is up. Is it OK if we stop here, Sue?

Sue: Yes.

References

Resnick, R. (1984). Gestalt therapy east and west: bi-coastal dialogue, debate or debacle? *The Gestalt Journal*, 7 (I), 13-32. (Verbatim transcript of keynote address at the Fourth Annual Gestalt conference presented June 11, 1982, Provincetown, MA)

The Training of Gestalt Therapists: A Symposium[*]

George Brown
Elizabeth Mintz
Sonia March Nevis
Edward W.L. Smith
— Participants

Robert Harman
—Moderator

BOB HARMAN: Good morning. For those of you who were here last year for my presentation of "The Case of Rose: or Will She Fit in a Toyota" [A transcription appeared in the spring, 1986, issue of *The Gestalt Journal* (Vol. IX, No. 1)] Rose sends her regards. She knew that I was coming and wants the people who are familiar with her to know that she's doing well and much better according to her self report.

Today's panel will discuss training and the training of Gestalt therapists — a topic that I've been interested in for a long time. I've done some quick adding in my head about how many years of

---

[*] This article originally appeared in *The Gestalt Journal*, Vol. X, # 2

experience with Gestalt therapy and Gestalt therapy training there are up here and I think it comes close to a hundred years.

I am not going to say a lot about these people. They are well known. George Brown is on my immediate left. He's an author, an educator, and an administrator. Next will be Sonia Nevis, who's been involved in training at the Gestalt Institute of Cleveland for many years and was the Director of Training there for several years. Following her will be Edward Smith from Atlanta who is active in training and has authored two books. Finally will be Elizabeth (Betsy) Mintz, a noted therapist, trainer, and author. We'll begin this morning with George Brown.

GEORGE BROWN: Thank you. I guess I'm an idiosyncratic deviant, and I'm not sure I should be up here, because I'm not involved in traditional training of therapists. We don't have an institute, and that's not one of my primary goals. I'm involved in two settings: The first is at the University of California Santa Barbara. I teach in a program called "Confluent Education" which started out by focusing on the integration of the affective and the cognitive domains, affective feelings, emotions, values and cognitive thinking, intellectual activity. That has developed and become more sophisticated; essentially what we're doing there is applying a systems approach to education. (When I say "education" I mean this in the broadest sense because we have people from a whole variety of occupations including industry.)

"Confluent Education" conceptualizes what happens within the individual (intrapersonal) and interpersonal and small group activities, the organizational context, and various instructional methodologies. And sometimes we design curriculum. I especially like that we see these things not as isolated components but all interacting. My major focus is on the intrapersonal and this is where I do the Gestalt work. I train, systematically, my graduate students — it's a graduate school I work in — in Gestalt therapy, making it very clear that this training is not for them to be used as therapists. Occasionally some of them, relatively few, do continue on and become therapists, but in order to do that in the state of California there are all kinds of requirements that they have to meet. So I don't have to worry that with the brief training that they get with me, people are going to go out and stamp themselves as Gestalt therapists.

What I am concerned with is how they can apply the principles, methodology and theory of Gestalt therapy to their own particular professional contexts, and those of you who are familiar with some of my books know that I've done a couple of books in education relative to that and I have one coming out, published by the Gestalt Institute of Cleveland, dealing with a Gestalt approach to organizations. Actually it's a way of conceptualizing organizations and working in organizations from a Gestalt point of view. It's an exciting, promising and rewarding approach and I encourage any of you who move in fields other than therapy to make use of what Gestalt has to offer.

That's one thing that I do. The second thing I do is train people in Europe in Gestalt therapy with my wife Judith. We work with people who are therapists, as well as social workers, teachers, medical doctors, etc., who want to have some familiarity with Gestalt and incorporate Gestalt in their own work.

— ON GESTALT THERAPY —

I'd like to sketch an overview of the sequence of activities that we go through, touching here and there on some of the things we do in our training.

We start talking about Gestalt as in Fritz Perls' terms — both of us were trained by Fritz and worked with Fritz — we talk about Gestalt therapists essentially doing nothing more than stating the obvious and making the implicit, explicit. Then we build a sequence of training experiences around that. We begin with learning to see. We do this in a nonverbal way through use of mirroring activities. Then we add hearing so that people learn to give voice feedback without words, like "dada dada" to catch the sound of the voice and to get out of listening to the content, for the time being. Then we put these two things together by adding language and focusing on stating the obvious: What do you see and what do you hear? We combine these. Then we add personal response. We build these sequences cumulatively. Then we usually emphasize basic Gestalt questions: What are you doing now? What are you experiencing now? What are you feeling now? What's happening with you now? Later on: What are you avoiding? What are you wanting? But not at this time. Those last two, we've found, tend to put people up in their heads. At this stage we don't want that. Then we do things like working with "top dog, under dog." We work with resentments, demands, and appreciations. This pretty much covers the first stage.

This goes on at my training at the University, but when we work with people in Europe we usually run a five-day workshop. The format is usually that Judith and I work in the morning with clients in a demonstration context. Then we talk about what we're doing as we work and relate it to the particular things that we're focusing on as we move through the sequence. We run mini-labs later on in the day where they have a chance to practice these things.

In the second stage of our training, we have something we call "pick a patient." We have a couple of chairs in the middle of the room and one person's a therapist and one person's a client, and we work on four themes. We work on the now, and that's to help recapitulate the first sequence that we've developed, because these usually don't run consecutively. (Usually people come and then come back next year or six months later, that sort of thing.) So we focus on the now, which again is related to stating the obvious. Then mobilizing energy, and we do experiments, like exaggeration, polarities, using your whole body, getting out of a chair and moving around, using sound, the voice, a variety of things.

Then we move into learning to work with the total gestalt, the big picture as you look at someone: What's the message you get? This relates to the last particular theme, trusting your intuition, where we help people to get in touch with various ways of knowing: learning to listen to phrases that come up, e.g., learning to listen to song titles. One of the things that happens with me when I'm doing Gestalt is I start to hear music and songs, and usually these songs have some connection with what's going on. Other people don't respond that way. They get pictures. They get images, metaphors, whatever. You learn it's O.K. to have these things, how to use them judiciously. Related to trusting your intuition we have a line that we say, "If I had the courage right now, what would I do?"

You learn how to become more creative as you use these particular things. Then we move into something that we call "mass Gestalt." We put the group in two circles facing each other (the inside circle facing out and the outside circle facing them) and we run a sequence of Gestalt sessions, some lasting a minute or a couple of minutes. In the first one we have the people on the inside become patients and they make some kind of statement about how they are at the moment. The person on the outside is the therapist and responds using all the things that he or she has learned up to that time. We give them a minute. We stop. The therapists move on. The patient begins again with the same statement said the same way and gets another response . . . so both the clients get an opportunity to see how different people are responding to them and the therapists learn how to respond immediately to whatever is going on. It breaks the old, going into your head kind of thing and interpreting, analyzing. Then we have two or three other kinds of things we focus on using that same format. It's very exciting. We also do some co-therapists, conjoint therapists work. We do a lot of processing as we go along. One of the exciting things that we've added in the last four or five years is what we call "the Cleveland approach": working in Gestalt from a group context.

People respond to this training with enthusiasm and with . . . we get lots of reports about how useful it is for those whose work is different from therapy. For those who are already therapists it adds a whole new dimension to their work.

One of the things that bothers me is the so-called "confrontive approach" to Gestalt. To me it's antithetical to what Gestalt is really about. Any therapist who assumes, even in an implicit way, to know better about what's happening with the client than the client, and this leaks out, especially in the quality of the voice, "I don't believe you," — that kind of stuff — when you do that it is antithetical because you immediately place yourself in a "top dog" role and we all know what happens with "under dogs," right? So we also spend a lot of time on developing a nonjudgmental attitude and values. That's all I have to say.

SONIA NEVIS: I tried to figure out what would answer this question, what was being asked of us, what I could tell you about training that would be interesting. I remembered that about twenty-five years ago we had Carl Whittaker came to Cleveland to talk about training a therapist. He said he had the same dilemma we are having: How do you train a therapist? He thought and thought about it. What he came up with is: You read the poets and the novelists and you go to concerts and you travel and you learn to play musical instruments and, if you work with adults you work with children for a while, and, if you work with children you work with adults for a while, and so on. He was talking about people that we all, I assume, would like to train. People who are lively. People who have interests. People who care about what is going on in the world and therefore are going to care about what's going on with someone else. If we talk about selection, we would probably agree that that's what we would look for. I believe that he was right — if training doesn't end up with everyone being excited and interested in what's going on then the training didn't take.

I've picked out three training issues of the many that we could talk about. All three have to do with what feels very important at the Cleveland Institute. Now I'm talking for myself — I'm sure that if I talked to each person at the Cleveland Institute everybody would come up with a different three. But I think it does represent something very real there at the Institute.

— ON GESTALT THERAPY —

The first thing important for training at Cleveland is it's history of some thirty years of articulating Gestalt theory, of talking about it, writing about it, developing exercises in it, extending it into working with the body, extending it into working with couples, families, groups, extending it into many other professions: working with the administration of public health and mental health agencies, organizations. There's been encouragement and support at the Institute for people to follow their own interests, so there's a body of well thought out information, well thought out theory, well thought out exercises.

However, that's not training — that is the ground for training. The training that goes on has to do with the practicum or the practice. The training has to do with taking all of that information and making it into muscle and glands and blood — well chewed and assimilated.

The practicum, starting the first week of training and going on again and again consists of people working as therapist, client and observers. The trainees expect to be looked at; expect to be talked about; expect to talk; you expect to question; they do not expect to be good. There's an easy-going ambience around practicum work that goes on for years. We remind our students that it takes a long time to take theory and make it a part of themselves so that they're not working from theory. (It's no different than learning to play a musical instrument.) When you first start you're doing scales, and you're counting, and you've got the notes, and you don't really make music for years. There is the discipline of practicing five finger exercises, and eventually arriving at the place where they're making music, where it's assimilated into them. So in that sense the training is a process that goes on over time.

The second important issue at the Institute is that we do everything we can, and have from the time we started, to make sure that introjection doesn't happen, that a trainee does not decide that one style or one person's way of working is the right way and therefore they are trying to imitate it. It's been very important for us to have a staff whose styles vary widely. We all talk about what we do exactly the same way, but our styles of what is apt to become figural, and the way we do our work is different. We've always tried to teach with more than one faculty present, and tried to get teams of people who are different enough so the minute a trainee thinks that one person's style is wonderful they see another one work that's very different and that's also wonderful. We downplay demonstrations because demonstration can be seen as the way one should work." We've even tried to keep the didactic presentations ever-changing — I don't think I've given a lecture yet that said the same thing.

We use at the Cleveland Institute a diagrammatic way to describe psychological process called the "experience cycle." It's been noted at the Institute — every time you hear the "experience cycle" described, it is described differently. It's simply not a fixed concept and our aim is to make sure that it isn't. We're not talking about introjecting concepts but genuinely grappling with them and assimilating them.

The third training issue is hard for me to say simply. It seemed important enough to struggle with how to say it, but I haven't been satisfied up to now. It has something to do with the general atmosphere at the Cleveland Institute, an atmosphere that makes learning, experimenting, trying things, lively and open. For example our own staff takes each other's programs. Everybody is into something new at all times. There is no sense that you can succeed or that you can fail. I don't think that exists there. There is both rigidity and anarchy, maybe because Ohio is middle America, we find we can go between being rigid (in the sense that the programs are laid out and one knows what the schedules are, and the curriculum, and things like that) and within that there's total anarchy. I think there's an atmosphere that supports learning there that is not easy for me to put into words but I think it's an essential ingredient of training. I think that's what George was talking about when he was talking about the nonjudgmental climate — it's a welcoming atmosphere for learning.

EDWARD SMITH: The training which I'm doing now differs considerably from the training which I started doing in the early 1970's, so I want to say a little bit about this evolution. When I first started doing Gestalt training, I did it through The Pine River Center in Atlanta. This was a group of psychologists and I was one of the junior members of that group. In the beginning we started with Gestalt training. Then we got caught up in all of these integrations with Gestalt. That was one of the periods in the evolution of Gestalt therapy. For a while it was transactional analysis and Gestalt, bioenergetics and Gestalt, whatever and Gestalt. That made sense, was exciting, and we thought we were right on the leading edge of what was happening.

Then I started hearing Laura Perls talk about the umbrella, how big the umbrella of Gestalt is. Then I was confronted by Jim Simkin. He challenged me for not having proven that I knew every-thing about Gestalt first, and asked what right I had to integrate anything until I knew all about Gestalt. So I thought about that. I didn't change much, but I thought about it.

I did learn something in the middle years of Pine River: we were overly inclusive. We were trying to teach too much, too many things. For a while we had three programs running simultaneously. We had a paraprofessional program for people who were not professional people, but were helpers of various kinds. We had a second track which was an introductory professional training program. And then we had an advanced training program for people who had already completed the second one. And, in both the introductory and the advanced programs we tried to teach Gestalt, transactional analysis, psychomotor and bioenergetics. That was in a nine-month program! Each quarter we changed leaders (there were nine leaders) in each group, with one leader having two consecutive quarters. So there was the continuity of one leader carrying over each time, and one new leader each time. We got a mixture of orientations (the thing Sonia was talking about) — giving people exposure to a number of orientations and working styles. But it became a hodgepodge from trying to be overly inclusive of content. The trainees said it was interesting, it was exciting, sort of like going to the circus, but they came out it not feeling enough depth in any one approach to feel competent and confident.

The next stage at Pine River was to stop doing training for a while. For several years we didn't offer any training. Then I started training again and did a program by myself. I narrowed the content considerably which worked much better. The difficulty I had was putting a label on it to describe it to people, to announce it ahead of time, because what it was — was what I did. It was my style of working which I think of as coming under the broad umbrella of Gestalt, but my particular excitement for the last few years has been very heavily body focused. So I called it "The Body in Psychotherapy." The training I do now has taken a turn, again, because I left Pine River in July of 1985 and now have one partner, Suzanne Imes.

So this has been an overview of the kinds of programs that I've offered. In preparing for this morning's presentation, I remembered a paper that I had written several years ago. This was an invited paper. It was to be a chapter in a book on training and supervision that was published several years ago. But when I finished the chapter and sent it to the editor, he wanted me to do some rather extensive revisions. He wanted me to include some material on the American Psychological Association's guidelines for supervision, and things like that in which I was not the least bit interested. So I didn't revise it, and consequently it wasn't published. That's a funny quirk about me. I've found I don't like revising anything I write. I love writing, but once I've written something, I feel finished and I want to move on. I don't want to go back and rework it and rework it. So I would rather give it one shot and get published, and if it doesn't go, stick it in a drawer and go on to something else. So I welcome the opportunity to now present this chapter. It's just been lying there dormant, just waiting for today.

What I put into this chapter were some guidelines that I have learned from the several years I have been doing training. These are rules of thumb. These are not, certainly, absolute rules. These are the things that seem to have worked for me, the things that I have come to understand about the kind of training that I do.

The first guideline is that the doing of psychotherapy is best learned by apprenticeship. As I look at psychotherapy, I think of it as an exquisite art form. I think of it as a performing art. And as such, to learn the doing of psychotherapy, one must apprentice to someone who does it. One must watch and listen and begin doing it, practicing it, polishing it. We can be scientific about psychotherapy. We can theorize about it, do research about it, study about it, talk about it, all of which I believe are valuable, all of which I'm interested in. But the actual doing of psychotherapy, as opposed to studying about it, I think is an art form. So that's the main guideline for the training that I do: I think of people who want to train with me as apprenticing and learning about an art form.

The second guideline is that in order for someone to really learn a particular way of therapy, a particular general approach to therapy, and to be able to perform it masterfully, that form must be egosyntonic for that person. That way of therapy must fit with who that person is, must fit with that person because any therapy system, any school of therapy is given life, is brought to life, through the person of the therapist. This is another way of saying what Carl Whittaker was talking about. That is, the person of the therapist grows and develops by playing a musical instrument, going to concerts, reading the great writers, traveling, experiencing, living. I don't believe that the Gestalt approach to therapy is for everyone. There are some people who just don't find a resonance with it. It's not egosyntonic for them. And it's a mistake for them to try to do it, because if they try to do it they are going to be doing something that doesn't come from their souls. If it isn't egosyntonic, then that body of material is going to be introjected, and the product will be similar to the product of introjected food. And you know what happens when you don't chew your food. From time to time I hear people identifying Gestalt therapy by the techniques, by particular, specific techniques that particular Gestalt therapists have used or have popularized. I remember the story, Bob, you were telling me over lunch a couple of days ago about some people saying that what you did wasn't Gestalt therapy because you didn't use a hot seat, you didn't have an empty chair there, so it wasn't Gestalt. Gestalt is certainly much more than techniques. It does include a body of techniques which have evolved, which have been developed. But that's not a closed list. That list goes on, hopefully. In addition to a body of techniques, Gestalt therapy involves a particular organismic theory of personality, which has roots in quite a number of people. And the part that is most often overlooked is that Gestalt therapy also has a particular philosophical underpinning. Gestalt therapy makes sense only in the context of that philosophy. It is, basically, a humanistic existential philosophy with a little oriental flavoring thrown in. Now if a person does not believe, does not have as a basic philosophical position something that fits with existentialism, some basic appreciation for such things as choice, responsibility, experience, then the techniques of Gestalt therapy make no sense. They are mechanical. I have found that sometimes I have trainees who do not go on to do Gestalt therapy, that the most valuable thing they learn in the training program is that this is not for them. And I am very satisfied when that happens. I think that's an important discovery and they go with my blessings.

The third guideline that I have stated is I can teach only what I know. I can teach only what I want to learn. The first half of that is a truism. Obviously I can't teach anything that I don't know. I have to be pretty well grounded in something before I am able to demonstrate it, convey it, show it, talk about it, in a way that is interesting, in a way that's alive, in a way that people can take hold of, chew on, and hopefully assimilate. The second half of this seeming paradox is that I can only teach what I want to learn more about. I think that one of the most important functions of a teacher, not just in Gestalt therapy, but a teacher of anything, is to be inspiring. There are two meanings of inspiration. One is getting excited, getting turned on to something. The other is, of course, (breathes) that kind of inspiration. That's the one we worked with yesterday. Breathing. And they're connected. Not just etymologically, but they are connected experientially. To be inspired is to be excited, turned on. And to be turned on, you have to breathe, you have to take in, you have to breathe in. And that's the way I try to teach. I like to teach. When I am on, when I am centered, that's what I do. I like to turn people on and get them excited, because out of that excitement people will move. Excitement leads to activity, to action, to movement, to interaction, to dealing with the environment. Now if there is something I am teaching that I want to learn more about, I will be excited, and then I will be more inspiring. If it's something that I have taught over and over and over in the same way then it's going to be dull for me. I am going to be dull, and my presentation is going to be dull. I perked up my ears when you were talking, Sonia, about "the experience cycle," how it's different every time it's taught. There's a basic core of information there, but the teaching of it is done differently every time. I call my version of that cycle "the contact-withdrawal cycle" in my book, *The Body in Psychotherapy*, and I have had that experience, both of teaching it differently at times and being excited and people really liking it. And there have been times when I haven't felt like doing it and I was scheduled to do it, and I would do it like I did it last year, and the performance lacked luster. So I want to teach whatever is exciting to me, wherever my growing edge is, and something that I can be excited about and turned on about. So that's going to be changing, that's going to be developing from time to time. Over the years there have been trainees who have repeated the program and I believe their repeating was more for the inspiration than for the information. The information itself evolves slowly, but the inspiration is fresh with each training program.

A fourth guideline. This one is one which I think has been talked about a lot and yet sometimes gets forgotten or neglected and that is that experiential learning is of primary importance. In our culture, the western culture, at least as far back as the time of John Dewey and his writings, we have known that experiential learning is more efficient, is more interesting. People learn better by experiencing things than by being told about things. So the main part of my training programs, the main emphasis, the main devotion of time, is to create experiences, to set up situations where experiences can develop.

Closely related to that is a fifth guideline. This is almost a corollary to the previous guideline. And that is that experiential learning is enhanced by cognitive structuring, cognitive framing. In terms of the teaching model, what I learn best from and what I prefer to use in my teaching is to do the experiential work first and then a cognitive framing of that work. There are a couple of reasons for this. One is that if you do a cognitive structure first, a didactic presentation, and then try to follow it up with experiences, people don't always follow the rules. People may not have the experience you just told them they're going to have. I remember this in a training program with the Polsters in La Jolla. They laughed and chuckled about this. They would do a lecture in the morning, about an hour's lecture, and then they would try to demonstrate those phenomena, but they would always preface their demonstration by saying, "Now this demonstration may turn out to have nothing to do with what we've been talking about." And, that was true about half the time. So if you do the didactics first, then the experiential may not follow; it may not connect. Conversely, by doing the didactic work first, you may be programming what's going to happen. You may give people the hint that this is what they should do. You may be inadvertently giving them a should in that and programming the experience. So by programming some of the spontaneity, some of the aliveness is lost. Just as importantly, doing the experiential work first then makes the didactic material personally relevant. And that's how we all learn best. We learn about that which is personally relevant. That may be the biggest problem in public education, in those years and years of school. I'm hearing it now from my kids. I have a daughter in high school and I have a son in grammar school, and they both hate school. And when I ask them about school, what they hate is that they are studying things, they are memorizing things, that have, as far as they can see, no personal relevance whatsoever. Now I learn very quickly, I feel very bright, very smart, when there is something I'm interested in and I read about it, or some experience I've had that I then go read about. Right now I'm turned onto whales. I went whale watching yesterday, and when I get home I'm going to read about whales. And I imagine I will feel very smart as I read that material. I'll really take it in because it will have some personal relevance, some relevance because I have experienced something now with the whales and I feel inspired. So if you can do some experiential work and then talk about that work specifically and relate that to theory there will be a personal relevance, and a connection can be made. If you do too much experiential work without cognitive framing, it's difficult for the person to transfer that experience into a new situation. The model is concrete work, concrete experience which then gets abstracted and filed away through cognitive framing. That abstract cognitive framing allows, then, a coming back down to, bringing that back down to the next experience, making the connection.

One more guideline. This is a practical one, and that is I have learned it is extremely important to keep the training contract explicit, to be very clear at the outset what it is that I'm offering. In the early days of Gestalt demonstrations, a lot of times very little structuring was done. I remember the first Gestalt workshop I was ever in was with Jim Simkin, and I didn't know what in Hell was going on. I walked into this room and there was a circle of chairs where people sat. He was out in the middle and he had a chair with nobody in it and a box of Kleenex. We walked in and sat down and there was silence. Nothing happened. We sat and sat and sat. It seemed like ten or fifteen minutes. It probably wasn't, but we just sat. I didn't know what was going on. There was so little structuring. I think that's a mistake in a training program. I think in a training program it's important to tell people what you have in mind, what it is you think you're offering, so when people pay their money they have some agreement with you as to what they're going to get from that. I think that's respectful. I talked a little bit in my workshop yesterday about respect. Several people were asking questions about doing body work in psychotherapy and some of the possible dangers of that: legal dangers, ethical dangers, what not. And one of the things I said is that the major thing, the major safeguard is to work respectfully, to be respectful of the personhood of each person with whom you work. And I think having an explicit contract for training is part of that respectfulness. That way people don't get disappointed. The explicit contract is a way of minimizing some of those implicit expectations. Remember what Fritz said about expectations. That can get very heavy in a training group when someone has paid several hundred dollars and spent several months with you, and at the end said, but I thought I was going to learn such and such. I thought we were going to do so and so.

BETSY MINTZ: What I'm going to do here is to tell you about some techniques which I have developed to help therapists — and also sometimes to help myself — develop empathy with their clients. Now as you know, empathy is not the same as sympathy. It does not mean feeling sorry for the client. Nor does it mean getting your own feelings all mixed up with the client's feelings, which of course is what we call confluence. Indeed, it is my hope that the techniques which I will present to you can enable a therapist to separate his own feelings from those of his client, while at the same time understanding and accepting the client's emotional experience.

Now, as we know, therapy walks on two legs. One is the intellectual, cognitive, technical aspect, which we learn from books and instructors and our own experience and which we may then try to teach. We can't dispense with this, but probably it is the less important aspect of our work and the more important aspect is our awareness, which I think is based on intuition as well as conscious observation, of what the client is experiencing at the moment. And technique alone is by no means enough to help the client himself become more fully aware of this experience. At any given point in therapy, it is always possible to use the empty chair, or say "Keep doing that," or say "What is your bodily experience now?" or say "Notice your breathing." Usually there are perhaps half a dozen interventions at any given time which may be useful, and perhaps a hundred interventions which may be useless or even damaging, like the example (which I liked) given by George, "I don't believe you," which I thought would almost always be non-productive or even counter-therapeutic. Our task, then is to choose which intervention out of many may be best, and this must be done in a split second of time, and the choice cannot be wise unless we are in empathic attunement with the client.

My techniques for fostering this kind of empathy have been developed in small supervisory groups of three to five working therapists, whom I see in private practice, since I am not associated with a training institute. In supervision, the most effective approach which I have ever found appears to be simple but very often — in fact, usually — has rather remarkable results. This is role-playing.

Let me describe this. Your supervisee introduces the client, usually beginning with elementary data — age, gender, how long in treatment, and perhaps the client's presenting com plaint. And if the therapist goes on, describing sessions with the client, it is perilously likely to approach what Fritz used to call gossip — that is, we are hearing about what happened, and nobody is experiencing anything.

So I say something like, "Go out of the room and enter again as Joe, or as Susie, or whatever the client's name is. Be Joe — or Susie. Feel like him, walk like him, speak with his voice and feel his feelings. And — this is important — don't necessarily try to imitate him but try to feel the way he feels. And whatever you do, don't break role. Don't give us little asides to explain your imitation. Just be the client, and I'll be the therapist." And I also explain that, in role-playing a therapist,

I am by no means trying to give an example of absolutely perfect therapy, setting myself up as a role-model of how this client "ought" to be treated. I am simply re-creating the therapeutic situation in order to give the therapist an opportunity to role-play his client.

Chairs are now arranged facing one another, as in a therapeutic situation, and I sit opposite a chair reserved for the client. Role-playing his client, the supervisee is asked to leave the room and reenter in role. And when the supervisee comes in, I say "Hi," which is my usual way of greeting my clients, and await his first statement.

Now, very often, something really extraordinary happens, and never do I cease to marvel at it. The supervisee becomes somebody else. His voice is different, his manner and gait are different, he even seems to be wearing his clothes differently, he has completely different mannerisms. Even the liniments of his face (or, of course, her face if the supervisee is a woman) seem to be different. You have seen photographs of great actors and actresses playing various roles? They look different in every role, and this is by no means entirely a matter of different costumes and make-up and hairdo, but also a matter of facial expression. The actual liniments of the face seem to change. I am constantly amazed by the dramatic talent shown by supervisees who, probably, have never seen themselves as having any special histrionic gift.

However, this does not necessarily happen at once. Very often, despite my explicit directions, the supervisee will break off and explain to me and the group, "I forgot to tell you, she just got a divorce" — or something like that. In this case, I say something like, "I want to hear it from the client. Go out of the room, come back as the client, and maybe you'll tell us about the divorce better that way." Or, perhaps, instead of identifying with the client, the supervisee will caricature the client, indirectly poking fun at the client, imitating in an exaggerated way the speech and mannerisms which obviously irritate him.

If this happens, we have already found out something — namely, that the client is irritating to the supervisee — but my practice is to put this aside temporarily and simply say, "I don't think you're really identifying. Please go out of the room again and really be your client and come in again." By now, of course, we are not using the word "client" but are saying Joe, or Mary, or whatever the supervisee calls this particular client. And, in role-playing the therapist, I am careful to use the name of my supervisee's client as often as may be appropriate, to facilitate identification.

Perhaps before we go further I should add that, in taking the role of the therapist, I confine myself to very general remarks designed to further the identification process. For instance, I would not suggest the use of the empty chair, which as we know often taps the deep unconscious. A couple of times I did try to get my therapist-supervisee to use the empty chair when role-playing the client, but we got such a mixed-up jumble of supervisee and client with this very powerful technique for tapping the unconscious that now I restrict myself to remarks which are designed simply to keep the situation going and to facilitate identification.

Now here's an example of the way this supervisory technique works, an example taken from my actual experience. Let's say that we have a client, a woman who is working with one of my supervisees in my small supervisory group, who is very compliant and does everything the therapist suggests. And the therapist could say almost nothing except "I'm really scared!" but reported later that he had experienced a slight trembling and an actual chill, a physical terror.

Now, what happened in the next therapeutic interaction with Sally?

Very little, in fact, that was really dramatic. Certainly the therapist, my supervisee, was too skillful to announce to Sally, "I understand you now, you're really scared" which would have been absurd. But there were subtle differences in his interaction with Sally, and in his choice of therapeutic interventions.

Within a few sessions Sally had acknowledged the underlying terror of abandoning what Fritz would have called the "phony layer" and what psychoanalysts would call "defenses," and to experience and express her authentic feelings. This was not dramatic, but it did mark the beginning of real and rewarding therapy. Dramatic moments do occur in therapy, but as we know they are few and far between.

We may speculate as to how and why this breakthrough of the therapist's understanding of his client occurred in the role-playing, a breakthrough which usually occurs — though not often so impressively — when the therapist drops his therapeutic stance, or in some instances perhaps his therapeutic mask, and identifies with the client. In this situation, I believe, a deeper knowledge of the client comes to the surface, but in my opinion this knowledge really was always there, though not available. In my opinion, we all know more about one another, including people whom we meet socially and not in the therapeutic situation, than we are aware of, a knowledge which comes in part through subtle subliminal clues — body language, tone of voice, and so on — and in part, I believe personally, through telepathic awareness. But this is a controversial point which we need not discuss here and which in any case is not directly relevant to supervision. Role-playing, then, is simply a method by which we can get our own selves out of the way and obtain access to our knowledge of the client's experience.

The example of Sally is one of many examples which I could offer you if time permitted, but it is by no means unique. Role-playing usually works. It taps direct experience, it's rewarding, and it's fun. Also, you can use it for yourself as a therapist. If you have a client who bores you, irritates you, frustrates you — and who among us does not have at least one such client? — you may be able to break the deadlock simply by imagining how it must feel to be that client. You can even go into an empty room and role-play the client all by yourself, although it does go better if you're with a colleague or a trusted friend.

You may find some interesting surprises awaiting you, and you may find your work with the client less frustrating in the future.

Now I'll go on to share another of my favorite supervisory techniques, although I like this one less well than role-playing. It's called, "Say what you really want to say." Here the therapist-supervisee remains himself, puts the client in the empty chair in his imagination, and tries to follow the instructions which I offer.

"Say what you'd really like to say to the client. Forget your professional responsibility. Forget that you're supposed to fill a therapeutic role. Just let yourself go, say what you really want to say."

Usually the therapist finds it difficult to abandon his therapeutic stance even for a few minutes. He will still try to "help" the client but will talk louder and be more directive. It takes several efforts on my part, usually, before the inner feelings really come out. Here's one example:

The client, Judy, was working with one of my therapist-supervisees who was irritated by her, and understandably so. She had inherited a little trust fund which gave her barely enough money to live on, but not to live comfortably, and because her income was so low she had persuaded the therapist to accept her at a very minimal fee. Incidentally, I think that the importance of the fee, be it high or low, is often minimized in supervision, whether therapy is carried on in private practice or in a clinic.

Anyhow, Judy had some secretarial skills and she was young and healthy and reasonably personable, but she just couldn't seem to muster up the energy to find a job. She thought she ought to find a job. She really thought she ought to do something. But somehow or other, she didn't seem to get around to it. She slept late, went to movies, went to beauty parlors. And her therapist, my supervisee, worked very hard for what was almost a token fee, with endless dialogues between lazy-Judy and Judy-who-wants-to-work, but nothing happened. So I asked him to put an imaginary Judy in the empty chair, with instructions to let himself go and tell her how he really felt about her.

At first, as usually happens, he was like most young therapists — older ones also — in finding it difficult to abandon the therapeutic stance. He exhorted Judy to get a job, scolded her for not doing so, almost pleaded with her — but he was still a therapist and had not really expressed his feelings. Finally we did have a real breakthrough and it went like this:

"Judy, you are a lazy bum. You are a drone. You are a pimple on the face of society. You lie in bed half the day, you go to the beauty parlors to get your hair done when you could perfectly well do it at home — I notice you can afford beauty parlors — and here I am working my ass off to help you at practically no money whatsoever!"

The therapist changed chairs, became Judy and said in a soft, pathetic voice, "Oh, but I have so little money, I can't afford to pay you any more."

At this fantasized reply (probably just what Judy would really have said) the therapist lost his temper and shouted "Okay, enough already! Either you pay a decent fee or no more therapy, get it?"

There was a long silence. Then the young therapist looked at us, half-grinning, half-embarrassed. "My God, am I mad at that woman! And to think I've been letting her string me along all this time!"

We now discussed what should be done, and agreed that Judy should have a reasonable time — perhaps a month — to find a job and pay an appropriate fee, and that otherwise the therapist would not continue to see her. He left the supervisory session feeling relieved and exhilarated, and reported at our next meeting that he had indeed been able to confront Judy, and that she was looking for a job.

Was there a sudden miraculous change in Judy? Regrettably, no. She delayed a serious effort to find work, and dropped out of treatment. She did, however, return to the same therapist seven months later, with a rather good job as a receptionist, paid an appropriate fee, and settled down to work. The dynamics of this therapeutic achievement are beyond the scope of this presentation, but it is my conviction that if we had approached the problem only in terms of Judy's laziness (presumably compounded of a wish to be cared for and a wish to control the therapeutic situation) the therapist would not have been able to confront Judy effectively. He was able to do so only after expressing and assimilating his intense irritation in the supervisory group. Because of his completely genuine wish to be helpful, and his starry-eyed belief that a therapist should not be concerned with money, he had been helping Judy avoid the real question which underlaid her job problem, the question "What shall I do with my life?" His confrontation, eventually, helped her to face this question.

Let me describe one more technique, which is less useful and less dramatic than the ones I've just described, but still I think it's worth knowing. It's a modification of a little-known projective technique called "Eavesdropping," which probably should be better known because it's easy and useful.

Here's the original projective technique; you might enjoy trying it with yourself first. Imagine that you are in one of those old-fashioned restaurants with high-walled wooden booths, so that you cannot see who's sitting behind you, but you can hear their voices. And they are talking about you. They know you, they are friends or acquaintances or perhaps just people who know you by reputation. What would you most like to hear these people say about you? Do this part of the technique first, or else your client may be too upset to do the other part. And of course the second part is, "What would you least like to hear said about yourself?"

Okay, now here's how it can be used in supervision when you wish to explore the therapist-client relationship with your supervisee. You say, "Imagine that you're sitting in a high-walled restaurant booth. Behind you, out of sight but not out of earshot, is your client and a close friend, a confidant. And your client is talking about his work with you, and the confidant asks, 'Well, but what kind of a person is your therapist?' And your client answers. What would you most like to hear him say, what would you least like to hear him say, and what do you think he might actually, really say?" This little technique often gives the young therapist new insight into his relationship with his client and into the therapeutic relationship in general.

It's pretty clear, I think, that my techniques, my games, do not offer my therapist-supervisees any new knowledge about their clients. In formal supervision, the supervisor might diagnose the client, formulate the client's psychodynamics, and tell the therapist what he should do. It is better, I believe, to help the therapist become aware of what he already knows about the client, which is usually more than he is able to recognize and use. Nor does this approach rule out the more conventional form of supervision, which can be used alongside my games if it seems necessary. The games are fun, they make the supervisory sessions come alive — and aliveness, of course, is what we're after in Gestalt work.

GEORGE BROWN: I just want to say, Betsy, how much I enjoyed what you had to say, how much I support what you say. One thing that I thought about, Ed, when you were talking, was this whole issue of inspiration. It sometimes concerns me. Those of you who have watched Judith and me work know we tend to be inspirational. One of the things I'm worried about when we do training, is that this may give a magical quality to our work so that people think, "Oh, what you guys are doing is — you know it's great, creative, and so forth; I could never do that." And I don't want that and we try very much to talk about, not only individual styles, which is something very important, but the fact that you can do this. You'll do it in your own way, but there's nothing magical about any of this. You know, it's basic stuff. There's a sound theory for it. You can learn it. That's one dimension of it. The second dimension of it is when people look at me as if I'm some kind of charismatic or inspirational leader, it puts a great deal of distance between them and me, and I don't like it. And so we intentionally (I don't think in a manipulative way), when we do workshops, (most of these are residential) we are with our people and we talk about ourselves the way they talk about themselves. So that they will see us as like everybody else. I think that's important.

BOB HARMAN: Sonia, would you like to respond?

SONIA NEVIS: When we were coming in from the hallway, we were talking about whether there was going to be controversy here and were we going to say different things? Well what stood out for me was how different we are, and how similar. Certainly you're not going to mistake one of us for the other. Our styles are different. We pick different things to talk about. Things that were important to one weren't important to the other, but there is no mistaking that we are all saying the same thing. There's just no mistaking that we're coming from a common ground in terms of a stance we take with other people, in terms of how we expect to treat and be treated, that the theory . . . obviously there was nothing said here that jarred me, that I would not say, "Well, of course."

EDWARD SMITH: I was thinking that the "time of the Guru" is over. I think that may have been an important phase of the development of Gestalt therapy. That was an exciting time in our country.

And I have some nostalgia for that period with the flower children and all that. But that's over. That doesn't fit now.

GEORGE BROWN: I don't think it fit then.

EDWARD SMITH: It was fun at any rate. And I don't know of or see very often that kind of charismatic therapist. I don't think there is much of a place for the kind of charismatic, turn-on therapist that we saw in the sixties.

GEORGE BROWN: That's a problem in Europe, though, because there are some over there. I don't know about too many in the States, because of the nature of my work. But I know in Europe there are some and it really bothers me. Especially confrontive Gestalt which you find a lot in Europe, especially in Germany.

BOB HARMAN: Before we begin answering the audience's questions, I have a few responses of my own. There was a lot of agreement among the panelists and I was thinking how Gestalt therapy sometimes gets over-identified with techniques and people miss the real essence of the therapy. There are some powerful techniques. I believe the first time Fritz Perls said to someone, "Put your mother in the empty chair," was probably one of the most creative moments in the history of psychotherapy. The second time he did it, it was technique. And because we're smart people, and we see things work for others, we tend to pick up on that. People who study Gestalt therapy need to learn a sense of timing, they need to learn in their training that there are times when techniques go out the window and you are with a person in the empathic way that Betsy was speaking about this morning, and for me that's what distinguishes a trained Gestalt therapist from someone who has picked up a few techniques. There are Gestalt therapists who are willing and able to be with the client in such a way that the techniques are gone and they are with that person, responding to them out of their own personhood and out of a strong background of theory. For me that's what training is all about.

I was impressed with what the panel spoke about. I was also impressed with some of the things that were not said. For example, when do we decide, as trainers, to ask someone to leave a program? What criteria do we use to evaluate trainees' progress? Might we ask a trainee to repeat a year or, as I heard Jim Simkin say, "Take a year off and then have your therapist write to me about what you're doing?" I would like to ask the panel members, before we get some more audience participation to respond some to these issues about when is a person trained, how do we decide that a person isn't suitable for training, how do we select people to come into training?

GEORGE BROWN: I'd like to comment on that. First I'd like to comment on your comment. I can't remember whether Fritz said this or wrote this, and because I'd spent time with him and also read his stuff I can't remember. It's all one big, amorphous gestalt. I think he said that using techniques is the last resort.

SONIA NEVIS: . . . when I don't know what else to do.

GEORGE BROWN: When I don't know what else to do. In terms of having someone leave the group or . . . this used to happen a lot more with me than it does. I don't know whether I'm becoming more mellow or what. I usually am pretty clear in terms of my response to that person that there's a lot of pathology there. If I had the time and the energy I could do it. But I don't have the time and energy. And it's not fair to the other people in the group and so it's very clear for me and I do it with . . . feeling a little badly for the person, but clear and clean, and I say to them, "You're not ready." This is mostly in the university situation. I had a case recently of a professor from a European country who came to be in our training, in our work, and in all four of our classes that were going on that quarter he was wanting to teach the class. And that manifested all kinds of strange and bizarre behavior. And I remember telling him to leave, with pleasure.

EDWARD SMITH: I think there's a prior issue to asking people to leave, and that's the issue of screening or "deselecting" in the first place. "Deselecting." That's a word I learned from the Peace Corp. I worked for the Peace Corp some years ago as a field assessment counselor and we "deselected" people. In a training program you have the option of deselecting at the technique level — deselecting or slowing someone down in the program if they are just catching onto techniques. Or, if, as I was saying earlier, the approach is not egosyntonic for someone. I think there are two issues here: There is the issue of technique — do the trainees resonate with what you're teaching or do they just not catch on, just not get the message because it doesn't fit with who they are? And the other issue is one more of ethics and morality. There are people who have a relatively neglected sense of respect for other people, and some of them want to be therapists. Over the years I can only remember our deselecting one person on that basis who was already in the program. There may have been some others . . . this person may be outstanding because we had a lot of trouble with him. He was a social psychologist who wanted to retrain in clinical and was taking Gestalt training but seemed to have a lack of a sense of appropriateness. And so we asked him not to continue the program. We told him he could not continue the program and suggested that he seek some individual therapy and begin exploring himself in that way.

BETSY MINTZ: The big controversy in a number of organizations that I'm familiar with is a topic on which I have no opinion — which is kind of unusual for me — and that is whether or not we should accept for training people with no background in one of the relevant disciplines (psychology, psychiatry, social work, nursing). I feel there is so much to be said on both sides of this issue. It's a very hot topic. It has practical implications because of the insurance situation and the malpractice situation and I think this has to be recognized.

SONIA NEVIS: I'm not sure I have anything new to say except that it's an issue that has been batted about over the years at the Institute and that we go back and forth between total anarchy and total rigidity. I remember a whole day when the staff got together to try to deal with selection issues and we divided into two groups, those who were "elite" and those who were "slobs." I was in the "slob" category. So I don't know. Selection is talked about — not decided about. There are things to be said on all sides. I agree with what you're saying, Ed, in terms of selection. I don't imagine that anybody comes to the Institute without somebody having known them previously, trained with other people that were known, or known other students. For people who are slower learners it's the responsibility of the staff to continually tell them that they are learning slowly and tell them what we think and tell them what we think they need. I don't think it's our job to control what they do and how they do it, but to stay honest to what we see and think. Thinking back over all the years, I can remember two people we asked to leave. Two.

BOB HARMAN: I'd like now to open the floor for questions from the audience.

QUESTION: I wonder if there's any ethical or legal problems in a university setting when a student is matriculated and already accepted into the program and performing adequately on papers and tests and so forth — I believe you can't flunk them out of the program or give a bad grade for having a bad personality . . .

GEORGE BROWN: In my university that is true. You can't kick someone out of a program, but each instructor has the authority to not take anybody in his or her class that he or she doesn't want. So, in effect, if they don't want to leave, we'll say fine, hang around, but you're not going to be allowed into any other of the classes.

QUESTION: I wonder if you'd deal with the issue of certifying or not certifying as a result of going through an institute training program? Why not have certificates for people who have reached a certain point in Gestalt training? What might that communicate to the public?

BETSY MINTZ: Well, I am unable to take a firm stance on this whole question of training. There's really no question but what some awfully challenging people may be lost to us if we require formal academic preparation and yet I have actually seen people who have never been able to do anything that worked out for them and they think to themselves: "Well, I may as well be a therapist." I've never been able to think this through thoroughly. I would like somebody to help me think it through clearly.

SONIA NEVIS: I have a strong bias. I'm very much against certification. I was against it all those years ago when they first began licensing laws in Ohio. Things change. Shapes change. I don't know what people are going to do and what direction they are going to take. I can't predict into the future who's going to develop in what way. And, I don't see that licensing has done us any good anyway. So I'm against it.

QUESTION: I've been hearing all weekend about how we as trainers and therapists have been evolving and the rules won't work and it's past. We seem to be implying that there is something new about trainees today that wasn't true before. I don't think that's been clearly articulated as yet.

SONIA NEVIS: I'll start. I'll start on the guru side and then get to how the trainee side is different. I think there are no gurus now because the very things that we are teaching are not mysterious. That's what a guru is — mystery. Therefore, all the power is invested in the person that's doing this mysterious thing. I don't think that what we do is mysterious anymore. I think those years have gone and that many of the things that we teach are now in the general culture. I think we've had a tremendous impact. So here we are. You know what I know when you're my trainee. Obviously I know more if you're my trainee because I've had many more years of experience and I've put a lot of energy into finding ways to talk about it and finding ways to teach it, but you're not coming to me for some mysterious things. You know very well that therapy comes from a certain frame or theory, a certain set of practices. We, the trainers, have some idea of what people can learn, how they learn, how much they learn. They know they're not going to be transformed. So, I think trainees today are different. They're very sophisticated compared to twenty-five years ago. It's dramatically different and the questions that are asked make teaching much more interesting and more challenging.

BETSY MINTZ: I'm very impressed with what Sonia just said — that the guru is now obsolete because we are no longer mysterious. I like that concept very much. But I think we must recognize at the same time that there are always unexplored frontiers and that if you ever believe that you have codified your approach to your patients and your knowledge of theory and your knowledge of techniques to the point where you just have to push a little computer button and out comes the right technique, you're dead. You have to rely to some extent upon your mysterious wisdom and upon the mysterious wisdom of your client and your trainee.

QUESTION: Should training require and/or involve Gestalt therapy for the trainee? Also, what's the difference between training and therapy?

SONIA NEVIS: Therapy has to be part of the training or else the training is nothing.

EDWARD SMITH: Yes.

BETSY MINTZ: You know, you could make a case for their being similar. I see therapy, or I like to see therapy, as helping someone grow up and develop, rather than us fixing up symptoms or problems, and certainly training is also not only the imparting of knowledge but the stimulus, the provision of an optimum climate for self development. And here there's a lot of overlap. I always resented having come originally from the psychoanalytic background. I was always infuriated by the assumption that if an analyst in training had any countertransference problems, back to the couch. You're not sup-posed to have any feelings for your patient. I recall when I was doing supervision ages back, my first supervisor said, "I think I have a problem with this patient. I like him." Now that's a little too far of a spin off of are they the same, but I think you are dealing either in therapy or in training with a whole, entire human being including both the feelings and the intellect, and if you emphasize only the intellect in training and only the feelings in therapy you're off.

SONIA NEVIS: I see it the same way. For me, they're totally different, and yet you can't take them apart. The image I sometimes have is of playing the piano with two hands. With the left hand you're keeping the beat. That's what you're doing in training. You're teaching people what the beat is and what to be aware of and what to watch and to get that sense of timing and rhythm. But with the right hand, the melody, you're being more authentically there, which has to do with therapy and of course what makes therapy so hard is that you've got to play with two hands. They come together and I can't imagine any training program that doesn't pay attention to both, all the time, side by side.

BETSY MINTZ: I would like to mention that I think it is almost always a bad idea to have the same therapist serve later as supervisor, that you get so imbued with a particular approach that you become narrow or perhaps you introject in the sense of swallowing without chewing. I'm always distressed when I hear that a therapist has been in treatment with so and so for so many years and then supervision with the same person for so and so many years. It seems to me this is deadening.

QUESTION: I'd like to bring up the issue of confrontation again. I was disturbed by the ease with which it was decided that confrontation is a bad thing to do.

BOB HARMAN: I don't believe we decided that.

QUESTION: Well, that was my sense. And I'm a little struck by the absence of controversy, argument, disagreement here. I'd like to know in your teaching how you handle the issue of aggression. To me, a healthy part of my experience at the New York Institute for Gestalt Therapy was dealing with argument and disagreement and restructuring, and rebuilding. And I really haven't heard much discussion about how you handle that in your training.

BOB HARMAN: I personally welcome disagreements and aggression and differences when it's done respectfully. I encourage that.

QUESTION: What is respectful aggression?

BOB HARMAN: It's when a person is searching for information or making a point or expressing themselves fully in such way that they are not trying to annihilate me.

SONIA NEVIS: Aggression and confrontation are not the same thing. Aggression in the sense of lively differences or aggression in terms of being very interested in something and pursuing that interest and mobilizing oneself and mobilizing other people seems to be just so central to Gestalt therapy that I can't imagine a training program or an institution without it. I joke that in Cleveland there are as many views of an issue as there are people viewing the issue. There's never agreement at one level even though there may be agreement at another level. As for confrontation, I called it the other day "cowboy psychology." Confrontation is coming at somebody aiming to surprise and startle and to get them off their center when they're not ready. It's not that I don't know the advantages of startling and surprising and not even that I don't do it when I'm in the mood to be mean — but those are not my proudest moments. I don't think it's intrinsic to Gestalt therapy at all, that kind of shocking, startling, surprising thing that I call confrontation. Again that has nothing to do with disagreement. There's plenty. There's plenty here on the panel.

BOB HARMAN: I would like to thank the panel for being here. I think your contributions have been excellent.

> *This article was edited from a transcription of a panel presentation at The Gestalt Journal's Eighth Annual Conference on the Theory and Practice of Gestalt Therapy which met in Provincetown, Massachusetts, on May 16, 17, and 18, 1986. The individual participants edited their own sections and Gestalt Journal Editor Joe Wysong edited the question and answer section and assembled the final version.*

Gestalt Therapy as Brief Therapy*

Gestalt therapy has over the years since its heyday in the late 60s and early 70s been primarily associated with a body of powerful techniques (Enns, 1987, Harman, 1989, Ivey, A., Ivey, M. and Simek-Downing, L., 1987). While it is true that Gestalt therapy did develop many powerful techniques, it is lesser known that these techniques grew out of an enduring and rich theory. In fact, the theory is so enduring that it is just as relevant today as it was twenty-five years ago. The lasting relevance of Gestalt therapy has enabled it to be applied to a wide variety of client populations, such as groups, couples, families, children, and individuals.

Now the question becomes, "Can Gestalt therapy work with these populations using a brief approach?" This question arises because of several societal forces. The economic climate influences to a huge degree the amount of money available for counseling and therapy. Personal income, insurance companies, HMOs, and PPOs all may place restrictive limitations on the number of sessions or the amount they will reimburse for psychotherapy. Now the specter of managed

---

* This article originally appeared in *The Gestalt Journal*, XVIII, No. 2

health care by the federal government looms on the horizon. Many community agencies and university counseling centers (Gilbert, 1992) have been forced, because of an overwhelming demand for their services, to limit the number of sessions per client and to adopt a "brief" approach.

Clearly, brief therapy is here to stay. What is not so clear is how Gestalt therapy fits with a brief approach. Actually, Gestalt therapy may have been the first brief therapy! In the sixties when Fritz Perls and a few others were doing Gestalt therapy workshops and demonstrations around the country, volunteers would come forward from the audience to work with the presenter. The volunteer would ask to work on a dream, on some issue, or perhaps ask to work on expanding awareness. Usually the Gestalt therapist leading the workshop had never met the volunteer and, most likely, they would never meet again. Some volunteers reported that these one-shot, brief episodes had a profound influence on their lives (Gaines, 1979). Could this have been the first brief therapy as we now know it? At any rate, the rest of this article will describe the fit between Gestalt therapy and a brief therapy approach.

Theory

Fritz Perls did not whimsically select the name, Gestalt therapy, for his radical new approach. Perls and his associates selected the name because of their respect for the contributions to the understanding of human behavior of the Gestalt psychologists (Perls, Hefferline, & Goodman, 1951). Space does not permit, nor is it necessary, to give a complete explication of Gestalt therapy theory.

However, certain fundamental concepts must be described in order to explain Gestalt therapy as brief therapy.

Figure and Ground

The way the human organism navigates daily through the environmental maze of possibilities is by forming figures of interest against the background of what is unimportant to the present moment. This process should not be thought of as problem solving per se, instead it is the ongoing organizing of experience according to the primary need of the moment. This organizing process is continuous and inevitable. Latner (1992, p.26) puts it this way, "It is organized in this way because our nervous systems can do nothing other than this. This is how we experience." Once a clear figure or gestalt is found, the person tends to it with regard to his or her own goals and needs at that moment. Ergo, the hungry person will eat, the thirsty person will drink, or the sad person will cry. That is, unless the person is dieting, has an eating disorder or had been told that only "sissies" cry. The point is that one will destructure or destroy what is figural in some way, either healthfully or unhealthfully.

When unfettered, we engage in a continuous process of figure formation and destruction. After destruction the whole process repeats until another figure is formed. On the other hand, people develop various methods of interfering with, or interrupting, or disrupting the gestalt formation process; or they may become fixated, rigidified, or stuck so that new figures cannot form. This is, of course, the condition of many clients when they enter counseling.

The point needs to be made that this is only a portion of Gestalt therapy's theoretical model. But it is, in this author's opinion, the portion that is most germane to a brief model. Readers wanting to examine Gestalt therapy theory in more detail are advised to read Harman (1989, 1990), Latner (1992), or Wheeler (1991).

Practice

Each Session as a Whole

It is possible, following this method, to do single-session therapy or a limited number of sessions around one theme or goal. The first phase of a session is to establish a contract as to what it is the client wants to work on. This may be done through such questions as, "What do you want to work on?" or "What are you hoping I can help you with?" and so forth. In a brief approach we must have specificity. If the client can clearly identify a problem, i.e., has something foreground or figural, all well and good. If not, this is where we start. For example, in response to our striving for a contract a client might say, "I want to work on my anger." This is a request that is much too broad to accept in a brief approach. The therapist could respond, "It would help me to know of a situation or a person where your anger is a problem for you." Some clients may be able to immediately identify a situation or person. However, others may respond with, "Oh, my mother, my father, my teacher, my boss, just about everyone." Can you select one of those that is most important to you?" the therapist may respond. It is important to keep the issue manageable for each session.

The particular configuration of each client's awareness will influence how easily or how difficult this first phase, contracting, will be. For some clients, their inner experience will be so unorganized, perhaps even chaotic, that it will be difficult to establish a contract.

Then there are the clients who enter into counseling clearly knowing what they want to work on, and contracting is an easy matter. Either way, the Gestalt dictum, "What is, is." (Polster & Polster, 1976) is apropos. We work with the client's experience, whatever that may be. For instance, the client with the unorganized, chaotic experience (in other words, nothing is figural) may be asked to get more into his or her chaos, to become as fully aware as possible of their experience right now. The intent here is not to make something change per se. To become more fully aware in the present is consistent with Gestalt therapy's existential theory of change (Biesser, 1970), that is, it is becoming more fully aware, more grounded in our present experience, that permits a steady step into what is next. In other words, the formation of a clear figure where there was none before. So the contract may emerge easily, or it may not. But that is acceptable too, because agreeing to work on one's present chaotic experience may certainly be productive.

The next phase, once there is an agreed-upon contract, is to bring to full awareness all that can be brought out about the issue. From the example previously cited, let's say the client, a young man, had decided that working on his anger toward his father is his most primary need. The therapist may respond with comments like, "How do you feel your anger? Where in your body is it located? Does your father do something that you get angry about, or are you always angry at him? How do you express your anger? If you don't express it, how do you hold it in?" The client may respond directly to all the queries and stay perfectly on track. If not, it is the task of the therapist to intentionally set aside these interesting possibilities provided by the client, and redirect the session to "anger with father."

Eventually there may be some natural finishing or closure achieved, or an experiment or other Gestalt technique may be introduced by the therapist. The experiment or technique is not intentionally introduced for the purpose of closure, although this may happen. The intent is to continue to clarify, to continue to stay focused on the contract, and to trust the natural process of figure formation and dissolution.

To continue with the example, the client may, in the course of the session, discover that he is holding his breath as he tells about his anger toward his father. He is asked by the therapist if he holds his breath when he is with his father and angry. "Yes," he responds enthusiastically. "Perhaps," says the therapist, "you are afraid of blowing over your father." Now fully in breath and emboldened by his discovery, he goes on to tell how in spite of his father's harshness he loves him very much. Breathing rhythmically now, he finishes by saying he feels better and he believes he can confront his father if he chooses.

During this session it was unnecessary to utilize any specific techniques. This is not always the case. Any technique that the therapist is familiar with, is comfortable in using, and is consistent with goals of the session, is permissible to use. Regarding each session as a whole implies that the Gestalt therapist will work more directly to provide structure and organization. It is the experience of clients that is unstructured and unorganized, perhaps even chaotic, not the session. By helping to organize the client's experience, needs may be recognized and resolved in that session. Of course not all client problems can be worked within one session. The likelihood of resolving something quickly is heightened by adherence to this model.

Here and Now

For years a hallmark of Gestalt therapy has been its "here and now" approach. Synonymous with present centeredness, the here-and-now approach of Gestalt therapy has to do with present awareness. This has never meant that we ignore the past or the future. Instead Gestalt therapists take the present as a reference point for the client to look forward or backward as the occasion warrants (Perls et al., 1951). But it should be noted that Gestalt therapists are more interested, as Latner (1992, p.17) has pointed out, "in the experience and awareness of remembering as in what is remembered."

A full embracement of the here-and-now philosophy is in complete harmony with Gestalt therapy as brief therapy. Translating this belief into practice produces Gestalt therapy's interest in the "how," "what" and "when" of our clients' behavior instead of the "why." Consider the case of Rita, a twenty-two-year-old junior in college. She asked for counseling because she was, "depressed and lonely, and spends all her time worrying about her ex-boyfriend." After negotiating to get a contract that was manageable under a Gestalt therapy brief approach, it was agreed upon that Rita wanted to stop worrying about her former boyfriend and get on with her life. Rita conveyed to her therapist that she spent "all" her waking time thinking and worrying about her ex-boyfriend ("obsessing" was a better term, thought the therapist). It was difficult for Rita to report specifically about her experience of "worrying." When asked, she fidgeted and said "You know, I just worry." Eventually, in the spirit of a here-and-now approach and wanting to understand Rita's dilemma, the therapist said, "Rita, I would like for you to close your eyes, relax and get as much in touch with your worry as you can, then make it verbal, worry out loud." Finding this easy to do, Rita recites a litany of "worries," e.g., "What's wrong with me? Why did he do this to me? He really hurt me! He is such a jerk. I'll never find another boyfriend." After several moments of this she pauses, grows silent, opens her eyes, looks directly at the therapist and says, "I don't need this. I need to get on with life." At the next session, Rita reported much less worrying and shared with the therapist some of the things she is doing for herself. The intense focus on the worrying, of making it figural intentionally, allowed Rita a sense of closure, or destructuring of that particular "worry." Prior to this part of the session, she was conflicted, torn between her worrying and knowing that she "should" stop.

This brief vignette exemplifies the Gestalt dedication to the here-and-now as well as our consideration of each session as a complete unit. In other words, this session can stand alone on its own merits, there is no need to gather more data, nor is there anything put off until the next session.

The here-and-now approach looks at the clients being-in-the-world. The therapeutic spotlight is upon the client's experience as it is occurring in the present. Emphasizing the here-and-now directly involves clients in their lives, provides them with choices, and makes them active in their living.

Experiment

The use of experiment is a well-known Gestalt therapy method. Gestalt experiments help to sharpen focus, to highlight what is, to restructure experience, to practice needed skills, and to add novelty to old, stale patterns of behavior. The most famous of Gestalt experiments are the empty chair and the hot seat. In actuality, the number of experiments is limitless, bounded only by the phenomenology of a particular session. More specifically, an experiment should always emerge from the content and behavior of a session and should never be preplanned, driven like a wedge into a session. In the case of Rita, presented above, the experiment was to "worry on purpose." Not all will end so spontaneously or so neatly tied up as Rita's did. Whatever happens becomes the next here-and-now part of the session. The Gestalt therapist will note if the experiment is accepted and conducted in a spirit of cooperation, "Let's see what we can discover about this." Some clients will accept an experiment compliantly, perform it mechanically, and gain nothing from it. And some clients will reject an experiment outright, saying they "can't" do it; they may ridicule the experiment, or say they would be too embarrassed. No matter, whatever occurs becomes the next sequence of therapy. Clients are never forced or cajoled into experimenting.

Experiments offer the opportunity for clients to learn, to solve problems through experience rather than integration. Reliance upon "experts" telling clients what something means, or what they "should" do is abrogated in favor of discovery, The discovery of the what and how of one's experience, or the range of possibilities for problem solving, and the discovery of their heretofore unknown personal resources, all place the client firmly in the driver's seat of his or her own life. In conclusion, doing Gestalt therapy briefly necessitates few major changes in theory or practice. One change is to stay on task, attending to the contracted topic, and postponing or setting aside those alluring side trips available in long-term therapy. Gestalt therapists rely on their theoretical understanding of the natural processes of figure formation and destruction to orient their work as brief therapists; restoration of this process is the goal.

References

Beisser, A. (1970). The paradoxical theory of change. In J. Fagan & I. Shephard (eds.), *Gestalt therapy now.* New York: Harper Colophon Books.

Enns, C. (1987). Gestalt therapy and feminist therapy. *Journal of Counseling and Development, 66,* 93-96.

Gaines, J. (1979). *Fritz Perls: here and now.* Milbrae, CA: Celestial Arts.

Gilbert, S. (1992). Ethical issues in the treatment of severe psychopathology in university and college counseling centers. *Journal of Counseling and Development, 70,* 695-700.

Harman, R. (1988). A response to "Gestalt therapy and feminist therapy: a proposal integration." *Journal of Counseling and Development, 66,* 487.

Harman, R. (1989). *Gestalt therapy with groups, couples, sexually dysfunctional men, and dreams.* Springfield, IL: Charles C. Thomas.

Harman, R. (1990). *Gestalt therapy: discussions with the masters.* Springfield, IL: Charles C. Thomas.

Ivey, A., Ivey, M., and Simek-Downing, L. (1987). *Counseling and psychotherapy: integrating skills, theory, and practice.* Englewood Cliffs, NJ: Prentice-Hall.

Latner, J. (1992). The theory of Gestalt therapy. In E. Nevis (Ed.), *Gestalt therapy: perspectives and applications* . New York: Gardner Press.

Perls, F., Hefferline, R., and Goodman, P. (1951). *Gestalt therapy: Excitement and growth in the human personality.* New York: The Julian Press.

Polster, E. and Polster, M. (1976). Therapy without resistance: gestalt therapy. In A. Burton (Ed.), *What makes behavior change possible.* New York: Brunner/Mazel.

Wheeler, G. (1991). *Gestalt reconsidered: a new approach to contact and resistance.* New York: Gardner Press.

Is There a Future for the Here and Now? *

History

The "here and now" was one of those catchy phrases identified with Gestalt therapy in the sixties and seventies and popularized by Fritz Perls and others (Friedman, 1985). Those early Gestalt therapists were, in part, by their developing of the here and now concept, rebelling against "talking about," which was rampant in psychotherapy in those days. Then, too, it was believed, and rightfully so, that important, vital behavior/material, especially that of a nonverbal kind, had been previously overlooked as unimportant. In spite of viable reasons for its emergence, the importance of the here and now as a theoretical concept became nearly trivialized along with other Gestalt therapy gimmicks. For example, the catch phrase, "I and thou, here and now," has long been a capsule definition of Gestalt therapy (Friedman, 1985). Trivializing of this kind led many to believe that the here and now was nothing more than a catchy phrase, as well as to

---

* This article originally appeared in *The Gestalt Journal,* XIX, No. 2

believe that there was little depth to Gestalt therapy theory. One purpose of this article is to dispel both of these faulty assumptions.

First, it may be helpful to trace the development of the here and now concept. Actually, interest in the here and now goes back before the publication of *Gestalt Therapy: Excitement and Growth in the Human Personality* by Perls, Hefferline, and Goodman (1951). For example, Kurt Lewin (as cited in Marrow, 1969) believed, according to his field theory, that behavior depends neither on the past nor on the future, but on the present field in the here and now. According to Lewin it is in the psychological present that behavior chiefly depends. Translating Lewin's view to Gestalt therapy means that the external situation, environment in more specific Gestalt therapy terminology) and how people organize their experience, is what determines present behavior. One's organization of inner experience includes goals, values, needs, feelings and emotions. This is what Wheeler (1991) refers to as the "structured ground."

The here and now concept first came to Gestalt therapy from Perls, Hefferline, and Goodman (1951). They pointed out ". . . . that whatever is actual in regards to time is always in the present. Whatever happened in the past was actual then, just as whatever occurs in the future will be actual at that time, but what is actual — thus all that one can be aware of — must be in the present" (Perls et al., 1951, p. 37). Even earlier, F. Perls (1947), in his book *Ego, Hunger, and Aggression* (1947), wrote about the past and the future, and the past and the present. What his first book did was to move the psychotherapeutic focus from interpretation to direct awareness and experience in the here and now. The founders of Gestalt therapy were emphasizing living fully in the present. One should learn from the past and thus make more adequate responses in the present as well as taking note of things to come and adjusting our present behavior accordingly. "The healthy person, with the future as a reference-point, is free to look backwards or ahead as the occasion warrants" (Perls et al., 1951, p. 332). So well before the halcyon days of Gestalt therapy in the sixties and seventies, Perls and others were giving thoughtful consideration to the concept of the here and now.

Erving Polster pointed out in his ageless article entitled, "A Contemporary Psychotherapy" (1968), that other movements were finding the here and now important before it was embraced by Gestalt therapy. He enumerated four distinct movements which were interested in the here and now: 1. Psychodrama, 2. The general semantics movement, 3. Rogerian psychotherapy, and 4. Group dynamics activities. Even though studied and stressed by others, it took Fritz Perls and other Gestalt therapists to place the here and now into the psychotherapeutic vernacular.

Gestalt therapists accept Latner's (1992, p.15) statement, "In its application, Gestalt therapy is a present centered approach." Being aware in the here and now allows us the conscious experience of being-in-the-world. Clients, in this way, can more easily consider their experience as it is occurring in the here and now, rather than by generating improbable hypotheses as to how they might have dealt with or understood their experience at various points in the past or would like to do something in the future (Spinelli, 1989).

There were good reasons for the development of interest in the here and now, which is synonymous with present centeredness. First of all, there was the belief that what goes on in the therapy session, that is, the interaction and the relationship between the therapist and the client was important on its own. Secondly, what the client experiences in the session is as important as what is talked about. Finally, there was the belief, especially as developed by Goodman and Perls from the ideas of the early Gestalt psychologists, that the organism continually organizes its experience as it interacts (makes contact) with the environment.

It is this latter reason that has been chiefly overlooked by Gestalt practitioners and writers. It should be pointed out that Perls and Goodman did not overlook this point and neither did Lewin and Goldstein before them. Of what importance is this belief, the belief that we constantly organize our experience as we negotiate the field? It is in the "here and now" (the present) that all organization takes place. That is, all figure/ground formation and destruction, all contact that differentiates the organism and environment, all exchanges with the environment, and all awareness occurs in the present. Once these fundamental premises of Gestalt psychology are accepted, it follows that the most fertile place for therapists to focus their work is in/on the present. This is where we believe we can have the most impact.

Application

The method most Gestalt therapists choose to work in the here and now is awareness. This may be referred to by some as directed awareness or even directed attention. At any rate, clients are worked with so that they achieve a heightened or more focused awareness. Perls et al. (1951, p. 75) defined awareness as ". . . the spontaneous sensing of what arises in you, of what you are doing, feeling, planning." The emphasis, in therapy, is on how clients organize their experience and to reestablish awareness of this organizing process. Full awareness includes awareness of one's motives, goals and values, and may involve us separately or in some combination with our sensorimotor, emotional, or cognitive processes. Our awareness informs us that we are remembering — now, that we are planning — now, that we are trying to manipulate, persuade, control, and so on — now. This does not imply that one must be vigilantly aware all the time, who would want to be, though it may not be a bad idea. But it is awareness that takes place in the here and now that reorganizes experience, and that reorganization leads to behavior change. Focusing, enhancing, developing and experimenting with the awareness continuum as it unfolds in the present is the arena in which Gestalt therapists work. But we have failed to avoid pitfalls practicing this way. Erving Polster (1987) proposed that we are "imprisoned in the present," and more recently, Gordon Wheeler (1991) expanded this theme by asserting that in Gestalt therapy we have become "figure bound." Both of these writers were responding to the accusations, and practice by some, that Gestalt therapy disregards the past and views the future as irrelevant. Polster (1987) went on to point out, as he traced the over reliance on the here and now, that it was easier to teach people to say, "here and now I . . . ," than it was to teach them to concentrate. He was correctly pointing out that in single-minded concentration, important experiences may be overlooked. While, on the other hand, feelings, desires, and values that are in harmony with an enormous background of experience lead to a rich concentration in the here and now that incorporates past experiences with visions of the future (Polster, 1987). So here we see the value and usefulness of the here and now, that is, it serves as a powerful fulcrum to connect the past and the future.

Gestalt therapists who rigidly adhere to the here and now approach have forgotten context and have most certainly ignored Lewin's field theory concepts and ignored the figure-ground concepts of Gestalt psychology. Wheeler (1991) refocused on the importance of the structured ground, that is, the total experiential background of the patient, including goals and values, from which present awareness develops that may lead to contact with the environment. And it should be noted that the developers of Gestalt therapy (Perls et al., 1951) were well aware of the structured ground, their book is replete with references to structure and figure-ground.

Polster (1987) has written about what he calls the "Arrow Phenomenon." He said, "Every event, whether as simple as a single word or a flickering in facial color or as complex as a policy announcement by the government, will point arrows into the future" (Polster, 1987, p. 42). This has to do with continuity, one here and now inevitably leads to the next here and now. The "arrow" that is selected depends upon our structured ground or how we are organizing our experience at that moment. Put another way, the arrows are determined by the prevailing need; which is in part determined by the past and the future. One here and now leads to another, seldom does an event just end and leave no arrows into the next event, into tomorrow. What Polster (1987) did not develop in his section on the "Arrow Phenomenon" is that in the here and now, arrows may go both ways, into the past as well as into the future. For example, most of you have had the experience of hearing an old, familiar tune; immediately you are transported back into experiences evoked by that tune. As I envision it, the arrows to yesterday and tomorrow from the here and now create a symmetry for healthy living.

By now it should be apparent that the here and now has a healthy future indeed. Moreover, if one accepts the view that the here and now is the vital connection for the past and the future, what we do as Gestalt therapists is broadened. This may disappoint the legion of professionals who want highly structured interventions and prescriptions for every therapeutic situation they encounter. And even more distressing is that they believe that there is such an intervention out there if they can just find it! At any rate, emerging from the here and now, as defined here, are several implications for Gestalt therapy. First of all, the understanding of theory in several areas will have to be emphasized. Gestalt psychology as it applies to Gestalt therapy is an area of learning that needs to be stressed in training therapists. That is, the application of Gestalt psychology via Gestalt therapy results in a here-and-now experiential therapy that focuses on what is — not what was, should be, will be, or could be. A plethora of techniques exists for the implementation of this focus. Another area important for understanding is the area of psychological development; this may include psychoanalysis, self-psychology, object relations, personality theory, and so on. Few would deny that in our practices today we are beset by patients with diagnoses or narcissistic disorders, borderline disorders, or survivors of some kind of childhood trauma, and it behooves us to have a theoretical perception of these dilemmas. Techniques and interventions should emerge from our understanding of theory. A good test for the Gestalt therapist is to be stopped anytime during a session and asked to explain how come he or she is doing what they are doing. In other words to connect theory to practice.

A second major implication from the understanding of the here and now as outlined in this article is that dialogue will increase and change. More time and energy will be spent attempting to understand the patient's structured ground and this can best be done through a dialogic approach that fleshes out the values, goals and needs of the patient in any given encounter. In this same vein, the importance of the interaction between this therapist and this patient should be explored. This is in the same line as Isadore From's (1978) idea that a dream, especially the night before or the night after a session may have an important message about the therapy or therapist. In other words, the manner in which the patient relates to the therapist, and of course, what the therapist relates and how the therapist responds, all play an important part in the here and now experience of therapy.

Lastly, it follows that if there is an increased emphasis on dialogue and interaction there will be a decreased emphasis on techniques. The stereotyped, rigidified techniques of Gestalt therapy are used more sparingly in this model. Resnick (1984) stated, "Well trained Gestalt therapists could give up all the well known techniques and go right on doing good Gestalt therapy." This does not dictate the eschewing of all techniques. We don't want to throw out the baby with the bath water! It does dictate less reliance upon technique and when techniques are used, a thoughtful discussion with the patient, including the patient's experience, of the results.

The here and now has a very healthy future. Especially when perceived as a vital connecting point between yesterday and tomorrow. The Gestalt therapy approach to the here and now revivifies the past so that completions and change are possible. It is appropriate to close with the words of Soren Kierkegaard (1954), "Life must be lived forward but can only be understood backwards."

References

Friedman, M. (1985). *The healing dialogue in psychotherapy.* New York: Jason Aronson.

From, I. (1978). Contact and contact boundaries. *Voices,* 14, (I), 14-22.

From, I. (1984). Reflections on Gestalt therapy after thirty-two years of practice: A requiem for Gestalt. *The Gestalt Journal*, 7, (I), 413.

Harman, R. (1989). *Gestalt therapy with groups, couples, sexually dysfunctional men, and dreams.* Springfield, IL: Charles C Thomas.

Kierkegaard, S. (1954). *Fear and trembling and the sickness unto death.* Garden City, NY: Doubleday.

Latner, J. (1992). The theory of Gestalt therapy. In E. Nevis (Ed.), *Gestalt therapy: Perspectives and application,* NY: Gardner Press, pp. 13-56.

Marrow, A. (1969). *The practical theorist: The life and work of Kurt Lewin.* NY: Basic Books.

Perls, F. (1947). *Ego hunger. and aggression.* NY: Vintage Books.

Perls, F., Hefferline, R., & Goodman, P. (1951). *Gestalt therapy: Excitement and growth in the human personality.* NY: Julian Press.

Polster, E. (1968). A contemporary psychotherapy. In P. Purseglove (Ed.), *Recognitions in Gestalt Therapy*, New York: Funk and Wagnalls.

Polster, E. (1985). Imprisoned in the present. *The Gestalt Journal*, 8, (I), 5-22.

Polster, E. (1987). *Every person's life is worth a novel*. New York: W. W. Norton.

Resnick, R. (1984). Gestalt therapy East and Bi-coastal dialogue, debate, or debacle. *The Gestalt Journal*, 7, (I), 13-33.

Spinelli, E. (1989). *The integrated world*. Park, LA: Sage.

Wheeler, G. (1991). *Gestalt reconsidered: A new approach to contact and resistance*. New York: Gardner Press.

Gestalt Therapy in the 21st Century [*]

It is indeed an honor and a pleasure to give the opening talk at this conference, *The Heart and Soul of Gestalt Therapy*, in which we are celebrating the immeasurable contributions to Gestalt therapy by our honorees, Miriam and Erving Polster. When Joe Wysong contacted me and asked me to give a "kick-off" presentation, I quickly said yes. I suffered only momentarily from what I call the Isadore From syndrome (1984), remembering that when From spoke to *The Gestalt Journal* Conference he told us that after talking to Joe Wysong he thought, "Why did I say yes and, what will I say." From went on to deliver his speech, "A Requiem for Gestalt Therapy." I am happy to tell you that we are not dead yet!

My first contact with Gestalt therapy was in 1972 at a workshop that Erv Polster led in a nunnery outside of Cincinnati. (There is something mischievously oxymoronic about Erv in a nunnery, Miriam too for that matter). From that workshop on, I have been enamored with Gestalt therapy.

---

[*] This article originally appeared in *The Gestalt Journal*, XXIII, No. 2

I gave my first presentation for *The Gestalt Journal's* Conference in Baltimore in 1981. Times were different then. For example, there were few if any cell phones or pagers, there were fewer gray-haired people in the audience, I was still married to my first wife, and we didn't worry so about political correctness. I am sure that if I told one of my many awful jokes that some of you would be offended.

Anyway, I shared my invitation to speak at this conference with my staff and told them that I was struggling to come up with a title. One wag suggested that I call it, "Viagra for Gestalt therapy" since we are trying to get up for the 21st century. I rejected that suggestion, thinking and hoping that we don't need artificial methods to get excited about Gestalt therapy in the 21st Century. Eventually I settled on the simple title, "Gestalt Therapy and the 21st Century."

I cannot begin to predict where Gestalt therapy will be at the end of this century. Will there be a meeting like this in the year 2100? Will there be a *Gestalt Journal* then? Will psychotherapy, as we know it, continue to exist? Or will From's (1983) grim prophecy become a reality?

Those of us in Gestalt therapy and any other phenomenological, existential approach are swimming up river these days. The river of treatment is flowing swiftly toward the increased use of drug therapy and other forms of psychotherapy. Psychological explanations of behavior are undervalued and biological explanations are overvalued. According to Shapiro (2000) biological explanations of behavior are simplistic. Biological explanations do not explain willful behavior, cognitive processes, character development, or the lack of awareness that we may find in many conditions. Drug companies and insurance companies are zealous in promoting a medical/chemical treatment approach. This is what I mean when I say that we are swimming up river.

How many of you in private practice would expect to be reimbursed if you submitted a treatment plan calling for Gestalt therapy or any other existential/experiential approach? Not too many I would suspect. I am not implying that I am opposed to drug therapy; there are times when I think that medication is essential to treatment. What I am suggesting is a balanced treatment approach supporting medication and therapy. And specifically supporting therapeutic approaches other than cognitive behavior therapy. (For readers interested in an in-depth argument against over medicalization, I suggest, *Your Drug May be Your Problem* by Breggin and Cohen (1999).)

Now I want to make a bold statement: Gestalt therapy should be the therapy for the 21st Century. How can I say this with such boldness, with such certainty, while at the same time knowing that this will not come true? I say this because our theory and method describes and works with human processes that are not going to change this century (or the next one for that matter). That process is that humans are always organizing their experience to meet or to not meet the environment at the contact boundary. We are always in the process of contacting, of interrupting our contact making, or we may be withdrawn. We engage in these processes with or without awareness or somewhere in between. Always this is the arena in which we Gestalt therapists work. This kind of human behavior, organizing and meeting the environment is not going to change in the next ninety-nine years. Along the lines of some things not changing about Gestalt therapy, I refer you to Erv Polster's (1966) article, "A Contemporary Psychotherapy." Polster's references to the contemporaneity of Gestalt therapy are just as relevant today as they were in 1966. So what has happened? Why aren't patients flocking to us? Why aren't therapists clamoring for training?

Most of you are familiar with the answers to these questions. I do not want to go into a diatribe about this so I will just mention some of the influences; some of the reasons why Gestalt therapy is not in the position that I think it could be in, in the year 2000. I have already mentioned the medical/chemical "solution" that many turn to. Huge culprits in this are insurance companies, HMO's, PPO's, and so forth. They are reluctant to approve therapy for personal growth or therapy to become more aware or therapy to learn more about self, etc. Our patients/customers are seduced into the myth of the easy fix that is medication and a suggested solution. Many therapists reflect the patient's behavior in this venue: that is, if they cannot learn it in a two-day CE workshop they are unwilling to make the commitment that one needs to make in order to become a Gestalt therapist.

There are other detractions that keep Gestalt therapy from being what it can be. One of my pet peeves is the way that Gestalt therapy is presented in textbooks. Several years ago I wrote an article in which I examined nine psychotherapy /counseling textbooks. I found seven of them woefully inadequate or just plain wrong. The only two books with acceptable chapters were the Corsini (1989) book and the one by Patterson (1986). Of course, most of you know that Gary Yontef wrote the Gestalt therapy chapter for Corsini. And I think, though I have not confirmed this, that Erv Polster reviewed Patterson's chapter for him. Some of my complaints about the other books were: 1) Little or no theory, or incorrect theory; 2) Seldom was the

1947 or 1951 book referred to; 3) Even Patterson is off when he states " . . . most Gestalt therapy takes place in groups."; 4) One author implies that the essence of Gestalt therapy is to have patients start every sentence with "Now I am aware of . . . "; 5) Another says that we "force a cathartic release in our patients"; 6) Another says that we play provocative games with our patients. Few of us would agree with these statements.

I want to complete my complaints about textbooks with this vignette. A friend of mine was teaching Theories of Personality in the psych department and asked me to speak to his class about Gestalt therapy. I thought it unusual, told him that I thought it unusual that a personality class would want a presentation about any psychotherapy. He went on to tell me that there was a short section about Gestalt therapy in the textbook and that his students were having trouble understanding it. I said let me read what the book says (it was about three pages).

So I read it in his office, finishing, I did not know whether to laugh, to cry, or to go throw-up. Finally, I was able to say folderol, balderdash, and excrement and I agreed to speak to his class. Here are some excerpts from the section:

> In Perls's complex position, the universe is seen as a continuous flow of energy and matter. Though a part of this flow, the human is nevertheless uniquely predisposed to comprehend what is going on. In attempting to comprehend, the human breaks down the universal continuum into bits and pieces that are labeled and treated as separate entities. In this fashion

are born the notion of different persons, things, times, events, places, parts of a person and much else. By playing with these bits conceptually, the human finds relationships among them and in that sense discovers processes. A process, according to Perls, is two such bits and a happening. It is in the depiction of happening that the basically intrapsychic nature of theorizing is apparent.(Maddie, 1995)

I could go on and on here, but you get the picture. You can understand why the students were having difficulty understanding. Finally, all three of his references contains errors, i.e.,*Ego, humor, and aggression; Gestalt therapy verbation; In and out of the Garbage pail.*

This gives you an idea of what we are up against. There are only three or four textbooks out there that we would accept (since doing my original research, I have found another well-written chapter, it is: *Theories of Psychotherapy and Counseling* by Richard S. Sharf, Brooks/Cole, (1996). In case I have not been explicit enough, I am talking about what I consider to be negative influences on Gestalt therapy.

In addition to the textbook fiasco, I would like us to leave all "Gestalt and . . ." approaches in the twentieth century.

In my twenty-eight year connection with Gestalt therapy I have seen: Gestalt and TA, Gestalt and NLP, Gestalt and self-psychology, Gestalt and biofeedback, Gestalt and hypnotherapy, and the most ludicrous of all, Gestalt and rock carving. In my opinion, none of the "Gestalt and . . ." approaches expand our theory or our practice. I am reminded of what Isadore From said: (From, 1984) "I have not as yet exhausted the potential implications and further possibilities of Gestalt therapy . . . I have not found it necessary to go somewhere else or to something else." I am not advocating being uninformed about other systems. As many of you know, Isadore From was incredibly well informed about psychoanalysis. Gary Yontef and Lynne Jacobs have written in-depth pieces about self-psychology. This may make for better informed people; I do not think that it makes better Gestalt therapists. In my experience, most "Gestalt and . . ." presentations I have seen, have been mostly "and . . . ," and have in fact weakened Gestalt therapy.

Another thing I would like to leave in the 20th century is the petty arguments we sometimes have and the disrespectful way that we sometimes treat each other. East coast, West coast, Cleveland, New York, Los Angeles, Germany, Italy, "I am better than you." This attitude hurts us. No one has the immaculate perception. We are all in this together and if we persist in the behavior I just described, we will most certainly make Isadore's prophecy come true.

I want to change my focus here and clear up any misconception that I am opposed to conflict or differences. I am not. Our theory holds that in making contact with the environment, we contact that which is novel, that which is different. I remind all of us of some healthy, respectful differences and conflicts that have been played out in *The Gestalt Journal* and other places. I think of the rich dialogue that took place between Miriam Polster and Joel Latner, between Peter Philippson and Erving Polster, between Gary Yontef and Gordon Wheeler. These are just a few of the types of differing I am talking about. Those directly involved had to think and rethink their positions. Readers were enriched by these dialogues. We need more of this type of differing. East coast, west coast, Los Angeles, New York, Cleveland — enough already. Everyone has something to offer. Novelty and differences lead to contact making. We need to be looking for ways to enrich and to support each other instead of putting each other down.

As a university administrator, I am asked to engage in what at times, seem like meaningless tasks. Specifically, I am speaking of terms like "quality management" and "strategic planning." One of the terms bandied about in the meetings that I attend is "stakeholder." Roughly translated this means "who cares." So if something would happen and we could no longer practice Gestalt therapy who would care? You would care I assume, and most of your patients too. But would anyone else? If you have trouble answering this, that leads to the question of how to expand our stakeholders. I wish that there were easy ways to do this — there are not. But I do have some suggestions.

First, do not ever think that your voice, that your caring, does not count. For example, I have already mentioned the Corsini book, the Gestalt therapy chapter, being taken out of an edition then put back in. I am not sure I have all the data, but I know for a fact that Joe Wysong and I wrote to the publisher, F.E. Peacock. Maybe others of you did, but not many. Now the Gestalt therapy chapter is back. What I am urging you to do when you see a chapter or a book full of errors is to write to the publisher and the author. You never know what influence you will have.

Another thing is to make presentations/demonstrations in a wide variety of settings such as your state and local professional associations. If you live near a university, volunteer to speak about Gestalt therapy to a theories class, to present a colloquium, to do a demonstration, etc. I have found graduate students to be a receptive audience and very uninformed. You may have to waive your customary fee for something like this, but consider it an investment in the future.

I would like to see more Gestalt therapy articles published in journals besides *The Gestalt Journal* and the *Gestalt Review*. I read some of those passionless, dead journals and I find that they cure my insomnia! Besides wider publication, many of the programs at this conference would be welcomed at state and local CEU conferences I attend. I do not know why we are not more active in these venues. I think it would give us more visibility and respect.

I am encouraged to see so many of you here. I wish more young people were present. Do you remember George Jones' song, "Who's Gonna Fill their Shoes?" That is what I think about now. We need more Miriams and Ervs, more Joseph Zinkers, more Gary Yontefs, more Joe Wysongs, more Jack Mulgrews — another Bob Harman wouldn't hurt.

References

Corsini, R. (Ed.). (1989). *Current psychotherapies* (4th ed.). Itasca, IL: F.E. Peacock.

From, I. (1984). Reflections on Gestalt therapy after thirty-two years of practice: A Requiem for Gestalt. *The Gestalt Journal*, 7, 1, 4-12.

Maddie, S. (1996). *Personality theories: A comparative analysis* (6th ed.). Pacific Grove, CA: Brook Cole. 81-83.

Patterson, C. (1986). *Theories of counseling and psychotherapy.* (4th ed.). New York: Harper & Row.

Polster, E. (1966). A contemporary psychotherapy. *Psychotherapy: Theory research and practice.* 3 (1). 1-6.

Shapiro, D. (2000). *Dynamics of character: Self-Regulation in psychopathology.* New York: Basic Books.

INDEX

Join the Gestalt Journal Press On-Line Book Club

Send your email address to <club@gestalt.org> with
"join" as the subject and receive a special promotion
code that will give you a 15% discount at the online
store with the most comprehensive selection of
books, CDs, & DVDs relating to the theory and practice
of Gestalt therapy available anywhere.
www.gjpstore.com

Explore the world of Gestalt therapy online and locate
a Gestalt therapist in the International Guide to
Gestalt Practitioners at
www.gestalttherapy.net

For a complete, up-to-date calendar of Gestalt
therapy workshops, training events and conferences
read *Gestalt News and Notes*
at
www.gestalt.org/news

www.ingramcontent.com/pod-product-compliance
Lightning Source LLC
Chambersburg PA
CBHW030645270326
41929CB00007B/209